Race, Class, Women and the State

Race, Class, Women and the State

The Case of Domestic Labour in Canada

Tanya Schecter

BLACK ROSE BOOKS

Montréal/New York
London

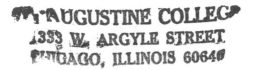

Black Rose Books No. AA260
Hardcover ISBN: 1-55164-109-7(bound)
Paperback ISBN: 1-55164-108-9(pbk.)
Library of Congress Catalog Card Number: 97-74161

HD
6072.2
.C2
S344
1998

Cover Design by Associés libres, Montréal

Canadian Cataloguing in Publication Data

Schecter, Tanya
Race, class, women and the state : the case of domestic labour

Includes bibliographical references and index.
ISBN 1-55164-109-7 (bound).—
ISBN 1-55164-108-9 (pbk.)

1. Women domestics—Canada. 2. Women alien labor—Canada.
3. Women—Government policy—Canada. I. Title.

HD6072.2.C3S34 1998   C97-900735-6   331.4'8164046'0971

**BLACK
ROSE
BOOKS**

C.P. 1258	250 Sonwil Drive	99 Wallis Road
Succ. Place du Parc	Buffalo, New York	London, E9 5LN
Montréal,Québec	14225 USA	England
H2W 2R3 Canada		

To order books in North America: (phone) 1-800-565-9523 (fax) 1-800-221-9985
In Europe: (phone) 44-081-986-4854 (fax) 44-081-533-5821

Our Web Site address: http://www.web.net/blackrosebooks

A publication of the Institute of Policy Alternatives of Montréal (IPAM)
Printed in Canada

Le Conseil des Arts
du Canada
Depuis 1957 | The Canada Council
For the Arts
Since 1957

Table of Contents

Acknowledgements

I would like to thank Professor Abigail Bakan for sparking my interest in the topic of female domestic workers. In the same vein, I would like to express my gratitude to Professor Elisabeth Gidengil for her unceasing efforts to guide me through clarification of my ideas and for patiently working through various problems associated with this work. By extension, I also thank Professors Hudson Meadwell, without whom this project would not have gotten off the ground, and Rex Brynen who not only fixed my computer at several crucial moments but offered unwavering encouragement.

To my parents, brother and friends I owe a great debt for their support throughout the period of time it took me to research and write this book. In particular, I would like to thank my father, Stephen Schecter, as well as Jennifer Moss and Vanessa Young for loaning me their editorial skills. Additionally, to my Vancouver friends – namely, Jennifer Moss and Doug Heselgrave, Jennifer Franks, Vanessa Young, Elli and Sahara Tamarin, Tamara Howarth and Daniel Rabibo – I would like to extend a sincere thanks for providing me, for an extended period of time, with food and shelter, if not wages.

Introduction

THE MISTRESS-SERVANT RELATIONSHIP

Clean the floor! Scrub the walls! Do the laundry! Wash the dishes! Cinderella, Cinderella.... always on the run. While most Western women are familiar with this classic tale, many tend to dismiss it as an out of date reality. Yet to do so ignores the reality of the majority of Eastern women, those living in the East as well as the West. This book examines the issues surrounding foreign female domestic labour within the unique context of Canadian women's history.

Since the nineteenth century, Canadian women, led by predominantly white middle and upper class women, have campaigned for rights in the public sphere[1], including the right to vote, the right to run for public office, and the right to equal pay for work of equal value. These rights ensure formal legal equality. They were won through a series of battles and are now hailed as universal. In theory, they help Canadian women to participate as equals in the public spheres of business and politics. yet in reality, only a select group of women can fully enjoy these rights. The policies that maintain them are predicated upon the notion of equality of opportunity, which means that women can be included in the public sphere as long as they do so on the terms dictated by male norms of participation. Since Canadian society is organized around a division of labour that maintains the public-

1

private dichotomy and holds women responsible for domestic work, only those women who can afford to hire replacement home workers have the privilege of participating on an equal footing in the public sphere.

As Canadian women have increased their citizenship rights and as the need for replacement home workers has increased, immigration regulations have allowed foreign women of colour to enter Canada in order to perform this labour. Yet these women are not granted citizenship rights and the conditions governing their living and working environment are increasingly restrictive. They enjoy no labour mobility rights, no collective measures for protection, and no civil and political rights. Required to live in their employers' homes, these women provide a captive labour force that enables predominantly white middle and upper class female Canadian employers to improve their status by seeking careers in the public sphere. It is at this point that racism and classism intersect. What is known as "the mistress–servant relationship"[2] is characterized by an intra–gender relationship of domination and subordination that is mediated by race and class.

Racism and traditional conceptions about the low value of domestic labour have dominated the history of immigration policy regarding domestic workers. Society views domestic labour as women's responsibility and assumes that it is a dona-tion they should make to the economy. Domestic labour, defined as housework and child care, is not considered a cornerstone of the capitalist economy since it is an activity that takes place out-side the public sphere. Its low status is compounded by the fact that its end products are difficult to measure. Yet, in spite of the "physical, economic and ideological"[3] cloaking of domestic work's importance, the labour force and the economy could not survive without it.[4]

While academics have paid considerable attention to immigration policies regarding domestic workers[5], lacking in the literature is a comprehensive and integrated analysis of how the State's immigration policy has served to reinforce divisions among women, how some Canadian women have had a hand in influencing this policy, and how this policy has influenced the

Canadian women's movement as a whole. In this book, it is argued that the maintenance of the mistress–servant relationship is aided and abetted by State immigration policies that, through the domestic worker program, subordinate non–citizen women of colour to white female Canadian citizens, thereby aiding the latter to make use of the formal legal rights they have obtained.

As well, it is argued that Canadian women, at various historical junctures, have played a role in influencing the State's immigration policy with respect to domestic workers. During the first wave of the women's movement (from the late–19th century to 1929), white middle class women helped, through their reform activities, to create the regulations that would govern domestics' entrance into Canada. At the same time, their reform activities and the basis upon which they demanded rights served to reinforce the State's perception that domestic labour was women's work, that it should be their unpaid contribution to society, and that some women, because of their skin colour (that is, non–white), were less desirable citizens than others. During the second wave of the women's movement (from the 1960s to the present), these conceptions were not fundamentally challenged. The institutionalized women's movement, operating within the framework of equality of opportunity, advocated increasing women's participation in the public sphere as the sole route to gender equality. It thus legitimated the idea that work in the public sphere is inherently more valuable than that performed in the private sphere while reinforcing the cultural invisibility and masking the economic significance of domestic labour and child care.[6] This effectively perpetuated the idea that domestic work is women's responsibility, while enabling some women to attain privileges, based on their race (white) and class (middle and upper), at the expense of others (non–white foreign domestic labourers). Individual women, acting as private placement agents, participated in this process.

Last, it is argued that immigration policy with respect to domestic workers has had the effect of reinforcing divisions among women along lines of race and class, as well as reducing the women's movement's bargaining power with the State. It was not until the late 1980s and early 1990s that the institutionalized women's movement addressed issues of racism, in particular the racist framework that informed restrictive immigration policies regarding domestic workers, and the traditional perception that domestic labour is not real work. Consequently, non-white and non-middle and upper class women, often limited to performing this type of work for other women, created their own organizations in order to represent their interests to the State. Ultimately, this has had the effect of dividing women along lines of race and class and of limiting their ability to demand programs such as nationalized day care which would promote true gender equality.

In order to demonstrate these processes, three distinct periods in the history of State policies concerning women and domestic workers will be examined. These periods are based on Linda Trimble's (1990) typology, which delineates three different types of State policies that are enacted with respect to women: policies of marginalization (mid-nineteenth century to 1929), toleration (1929 to 1967) and inclusion (1967 to the present).[7] Each will be considered through an in-depth examination of the complex dynamic that characterizes the relationship between the improvement in Canadian women's status and the concurrent decrease of foreign domestic workers' rights.

Chapter one covers the period termed marginalization which began in the mid-nineteenth century and ended in 1929 when women were recognized in the eyes of the law as persons. According to Trimble (1990), Canadian society was marked by a definite contrast between the public and the private during this period. The public sphere, which encompassed politics and business, was entirely dominated by men. The private sphere of the family and the home was the domain of women. Qualities such as altruism, devotion and caring were not only associated with the private sphere but came to define women themselves. Indeed, women were so strongly identified with the private sphere that their participation in the public domain became a contradiction in terms. This binary opposition of men/women, public/private was entrenched in law. Any hope of women's transcending the private sphere was ruled out by legislative policies that refused to recognize women as persons under the law. In essence, State policies echoed the social marginalization of women by recognizing them as objects of State policy, but not as active participants in it.

At this time, neither female employers nor domestic workers possessed any rights in the formal legal sense; both groups of women were confined to the private sphere. Yet white middle and upper class women, because of their race and class, were more privileged than other women: they did not have to work outside the home and they could afford to hire domestic workers, which in turn enabled them to participate in activities outside the home. Black Canadian women were forced to work in domestic service since racism made alternate avenues of work unavailable to them. Yet because demand for domestic workers exceeded supply, Canada was forced to recruit foreign domestic workers. This recruitment process was largely in the hands of white middle and upper class women who cooperated with their counterparts in Britain, through a series of private networks, to ensure a steady supply of "...the best classes of British [young] women".[8] Although initially imported to work as domestics, these women were slated to eventually become mothers who would help build the Canadian nation. Black women were largely excluded from immigrating through this program.

These white middle class Canadian women engaged in a number of reform activities geared towards achieving the goal of race purity.[9] These activities left a standing legacy in Canadians' collective frame of reference about the type of person (that is, white) that was both desirable and deserving of citizenship rights. As an outgrowth of these activities, the reformers came to dominate the first wave of the women's movement[10] which pressed the State for the right to vote. The basis upon which they made this demand, however, reinforced the perception that domestic work was women's responsibility and that it was the unpaid contribution that women should make to society. Although their demand was met in 1918, women were marginalized until 1929 when they gained legal personhood. With these rights secured, their position shifted to one of toleration.

Chapter two examines the period of women's toleration in the public sphere which lasted from 1930 until 1967. According to Trimble (1990), policies of toleration were rooted in the idea of extending existing civil rights (which were the exclusive domain of men) to women. Policies of toleration did nothing to challenge the ingrained gender stereotypes which served as a defining force in Canadian society. Hence, policies of toleration allowed women's participation in the public sphere to be endured but certainly not accepted. This period witnessed the removal of legal barriers to women's participation but lacked legislative policies that would actively include women.

The granting of formal legal rights to women signalled the acknowledgment of women as individuals in their own right. Although this was clearly a legal milestone, in practice it made little difference to the fundamental division of spheres. This policy change was significant in that it allowed women a foot in the door of the public sphere. However, once in the door, women encountered a new realm of unlegislated barriers to their participation. Those women who did seek to participate in the public sphere were seen as aberrant, and were therefore barely tolerated by men. As well, because women's association with the private sphere remained unchallenged, they were only considered qualified to speak on those issues which concerned the private realm. Lastly, policies of toleration were far from inclusive insofar as women were concerned. Increasing women's role in the private sphere involved only the removal legislative barriers; no attempt was made to facilitate their increased participation. Women remained responsible for the private domain. No consideration was given to the less obvious barriers, such as society's attitudes, and any discrepancy between men and women's participation served to confirm the assumption that women had no place in the public sphere.

Thus middle and upper class Canadian women remained largely in the domestic sphere while middle class British women with some education and skills, constrained by similar factors in their home country, continued to emigrate as domestic workers. In the 1940s the nature of the Canadian State began to alter from one which operated according to a strict division between the public and private spheres, with State policies solely directed towards the public sphere, to one that extended intervention into various areas that had hitherto belonged strictly to the private domain, such as health care. The Keynesian Welfare State was developing and new measures for workers' collective protection (Unemployment Insurance, Canada Pension Plan, and so on) as well as a new array of citizenship entitlement rights were instituted. But child care, framed within the discourse of private requirements versus broad economic and social ones[11], lay outside the State's purview insofar as these collective protection and entitlement rights were concerned.

New economic sectors emerged, and by the end of the Second World War, several new occupational categories for women opened up. Many of the women traditionally employed as domestic servants left their employment for jobs in these new sectors where remuneration was higher, hours of work better defined, and where protective measures applied. The Canadian State was left with a mandate to find a new source of domestic workers as Canadian black women and women from the traditional source countries were no longer willing to fill these positions.

This led, in 1947, to a marked change in the Canadian State's immigration policy concerning domestic workers. The State turned to other "less desirable" (that is, non–British) countries for domestic workers and simultaneously changed the regulations that had governed the entrance of women who filled this occupational category. A series of measures, gradually enacted as part of the immigration procedure, effectively restructured the system so as to ensure that the employee–employer relationship was even more inequitably biased in favor of the employer. This was largely done by forcing domestics to serve a term of bondage – in other words, denying them labour mobility rights – for a preset amount of time and by denying them collective measures for protection. These restrictive regulations were strictly enforced and further modified by the time Canada permitted black Caribbean women to enter as domestics in 1955. Entering on limited quotas, these women had subjective and selective admission criteria imposed on them, and worked under the constant threat of expulsion should they be found to be "unsuitable". British women who immigrated as domestics enjoyed full citizenship rights. Thus different policies were enacted in keeping with traditional racist assumptions of who was a desirable and deserving citizen.

During the 1950s, increasing numbers of Canadian women, including wives and mothers, worked in the paid public sphere. The numbers of women completing high school rose and many went on to attend university or professional programs.[12] As a culmination of these changes, Canadian women began to organize; the second wave of the women's movement was underway. Middle and upper class white women geared their energies towards instituting a royal commission on the status of women. With its creation in 1967, State policies governing women's position of toleration ended and women came to occupy a position of inclusion.

Chapter three covers this period of inclusion that began in 1967 and continues to this day. According to Trimble (1990), the beginning of this period was marked by the State's formulation of policies of inclusion. Policies of inclusion seek gender equality through the realization of equality of opportunity, addressing both the public and the private sphere. These policies accept the public–private dichotomy but also accept that women have rights and responsibilities in the public sphere. They aim to achieve gender equality by providing women with certain rights concerning their private roles (accessible abortion, child tax credits) and by legally removing barriers in the public sphere (legislating against discrimination in the workplace and education).

Policies of inclusion recognize that societal impediments have become systemic. While these policies attempt to remove systemic barriers, they do not challenge the underlying structure that made these barriers initially possible. The private sphere is still the domain of women, and it is still valued far less than the public, male sphere. Women who participate in the public sphere have two options. They may reject the private sphere and embrace the public sphere entirely, or they may employ someone else to perform their private responsibilities in their place. Clearly, this option is only available to financially privileged women. Either situation calls for women to emulate men in order to participate fully in the public sphere.

Although women of colour and lower class women formed part of the women's movement, they occupied a peripheral position. It was largely middle and upper class white women, forming the basis of institutionalized feminism, who managed to influence State policy concerning women. These women were at the core of the National Action Committee which, operating as an umbrella group, came to be perceived by policy makers as the voice of Canadian women. This organization worked from within the liberal feminist perspective of equality of opportunity and thus did not challenge the gender basis of Canada's social organization – that is, the public–private divide and its attendant value segregation. It did not demand a system of nationalized day care or support wages for housework. Nor, until the late 1980s, did it begin to challenge the racism that limited non–white women's ability to achieve gender equality and foreign domestic workers' ability to attain citizenship status.

While Canadian women were making advances in the political and economic arenas, domestic workers' rights continued to be curtailed. Although 1967 was heralded as a new era in immigration, the implementation of an ostensibly universal point system meant that domestic workers from the Caribbean continued to enter on a temporary employment visa system that treated black women differently than than it did white women. These policies progressively eliminated Caribbean women's chances to obtain immigrant status, thereby restricting their occupational mobility while increasing their dependence on their employers who continued to be, largely, white middle and upper class women. By 1976, these domestics were denied the right to apply for landed status from within Canada and, as non–immigrants, were required to leave Canada upon completion of their work contract. By the end of the 1970s, Caribbean domestic workers, emulating Canadian women, began to organize in an attempt to press the State for more equitable legislation. At this point, Canada shifted from the Caribbean to the Philippines as the main source country for domestic labour, and it became increasingly difficult for Caribbean women to enter Canada through the domestic worker program. This process was aided by female private placement agency owners, managers, operators and agents.

By 1980, a shortage of domestic labour was a constant problem for employers and for the State. The women's movement's demands for equity legislation were also on the rise. At the same time, the ideology that informed State action was undergoing a transformation. The collectivist ideology that had guided the creation of previous State policies was changing in the direction of neoliberalism – that is, there was a desire to trim the welfare State and the amount of entitlements that citizens could claim. This transformation was still underway at the end of the decade.

This had several implications for both the women's movement and domestic workers. Although the institutionalized women's movement had begun to realize its class and race biases and to redress these inequities, it could not push for more inclusive legislation (that is, legislation that would be class and race sensitive) as it was forced to defend and protect the legislative and service gains that had already been achieved. Issues such as nationalized day care were placed on the organization's back-burner. The retraction of the welfare State made "the crisis in the domestic sphere"[13] more acute. Women had to pick up the slack and the State facilitated their task by ensuring that immigrant domestic workers stayed in their jobs. This resulted in more restrictive guidelines regarding domestic workers: they were forced to enter on temporary employment authorizations and remain in domestic service for a period of two years before they could be considered for landed status; they were required to live in their employers' homes; and they were not granted labour mobility rights. These new restrictions were consistent with the neoliberal ideology that came to govern State policy. They enabled some Canadian women to take care of *their* domestic problem privately.

This analysis of the mistress-servant relationship is informed by a socialist feminist perspective. Socialist feminists[14] have attempted to engage in a holistic debate with respect to the source of women's subordinate status. Socialist feminism argues that gender oppression must be examined within the context of race and class oppression. Its premise is that the system of oppression that ensures women's subordinate status must be seen as the complex culmination of separate systems of race, class and gender oppression. Analysis that gives gender primary consideration and merely adds on discourse regarding race and class ignores the complex interplay between these three factors. Often, this sort of analysis results in the further marginalization of women of a less privileged race and class. According to socialist feminists, only by taking a holistic view can we understand the unifying and divisive factors at play in women's lives.

To grasp what conditions gave birth to the mistress–servant relationship, it is also important to understand the role of the State. As Randall (1988) points out, the State plays a vital role in determining and reacting to the economic, political and social forces that combine to forge women's subordinate status. State policies are born of a social ideology regarding women's place in society. This ideology is impacted by ideas regarding the race and class to which women belong. Hence, these policies affect different groups of women in diverse ways. The ideology that informs State policy has a very real manifestation in the form of schools or administrative agencies, for example, that shape women's lives.[15] Socialist feminist theory asserts that in order to construct an egalitarian society, one must first understand the role of the State in perpetuating oppression.

Although the historical process of subordinating foreign domestic workers to Canadian female employers could be examined from a number of feminist theoretical perspectives, socialist feminism is the only strand that is useful in examining the intersection of race, class and gender oppression. The liberal, radical and Marxist feminist strands inadequately account for the complex dynamic arising from the intersection of race, class and gender oppression that is played out within the mistress–servant relationship when Canadian women employ foreign women of colour as domestic workers.

Liberal feminist theory originated in the eighteenth century with Mary Wollstonecraft's *A Vindication of the Rights of Women*. She argued that in order for women to achieve equality with and independence from men, they require equal rights in the form of civil liberties and education.[16] To this day, liberal feminism continues in this tradition that is based on liberalism's ideology of individual rights. Liberal feminists[17] argue that women can achieve equality with men if they are included in existing political and economic structures. Consequently, all that is required is equality of opportunity. Once gender stereotyping is eliminated, women will be included on an equal footing in the existing structures of the State and society.

Liberal feminist analysis alone is inadequate to explain the mistress–servant relationship that is prevalent within Canadian society. Not only is it unable to account for the class inequalities that limit some women's ability to participate fully and/or equally in the paid labour force, but it cannot account for the necessity of subordinating some women (usually lower class women of colour) to others (generally white middle and upper class women) as replacement home workers. If gender equality is simply a matter of equality of opportunity, then all women should be equally able to access the public sphere and be equally able to attain gender parity. Liberal feminism ignores the ideological and functional roles that class, race and the public-private divide have in structuring Canadian society. By treating the problem as one of limited access, it unwittingly reinforces divisions among women along lines of race and class and limits women's ability to foster solidarity along gender lines, since many of the inclusionary policies that are advocated tend to be zero–sum: a woman can benefit from them only if she can find another (woman) to take care of her private sphere duties.

Radical feminists[18], on the other hand, believe that women's subordination is a universal feature of all societies and that patriarchy is an all–encompassing system from which every other source of oppression originates. Consequently, women are a unique class whose membership is defined by biological sex and who, despite differences arising from race or class, are bound to each other by the primacy of gender oppression. Therefore, women are perceived to have more in common with all other women than with men of their own race or class. This commonality of interest among women is the basis upon which women, defined as a class, will be able to fight their domination.

Marxist feminists[19] argue in a different vein. They believe that women's oppression is tied to the system of capitalist accumulation. Capitalism is not merely a system of exchange, but one that involves power relations. Several facets of women's subordination arise from this system. First, the public–private divide assigns women responsibility for domestic work. Since their labour power in the home is not remunerated, women are oppressed. Second, women are responsible for work in the private sphere and so are unable to enter the paid productive sphere to the same degree as men. As a result, they are subjected to more exploitation than men as they rarely possess comparable bargaining power (in the form of skills) that would enable them to attain higher wages. Last, because women are responsible for work in the domestic arena, they are largely unable to own the means of production. Consequently, all women are oppressed as a result of the sexual division of labour, and all women will be liberated from gender oppression by entering the paid productive force.

By stating that all other sources of oppression originate from gender oppression, that is women's oppression by men, radical feminist theory ignores intra–gender relationships that are characterized by oppression and domination. It also ignores the fact that some women, privileged as a result of their race and class, are active in shaping and maintaining these relationships in order to preserve their privileges. Marxist feminists, on the other hand, ignore the fact that most women entering the paid labour force are still not equal to men. For many women (depending on their race and class) entering the labour force has resulted in a double burden. Both of these strands of feminist theory, by treating women as a homogeneous group suffering from a single form of oppression, ignore the differences in oppression that arise as a result of race and class. Consequently, both are inadequate to explain the dynamics of domination and oppression that are played out within the mistress–servant relationship.

By applying a socialist feminist analysis to the issue of domestic workers and women's status, and by applying the analysis to three distinct historical periods, several purposes are served. First, a comparative historical perspective allows for a detailed analysis of how State policies regarding the women's movement and domestic workers are connected, linking positive ones in the former category to negative ones in the latter. Second, a comparative historical perspective allows us to see how groups of women, as well as the organized women's movement, have played a role in shaping immigration policy with respect to domestic workers. This, in turn, allows for an assessment of how domestic worker policy has reinforced divisions among women based on race and class.

Third, it is possible to see how the reinforcement of the race and class divisions among women has affected the form of the organized women's movement's demands. Specifically, by examining the history of domestic worker policy, it is possible to assess why policies of transformation were never formally advocated and how their proponents were marginalized from the political debate surrounding Canadian women's rights. According to Trimble (1990), transformative policies are predicated upon a belief that societal attitudes and institutions related to the public-private divide should be divorced from gender. These policies, unlike policies of inclusion, are not predicated on the idea that women should be integrated into the public sphere but rather on the notion of a fundamental restructuring of values such that the private sphere, and its attendant roles and duties, are no longer valued less than the public sphere. An example of such a type of policy would be fully-subsidized nationalized day care established on the belief that child care is society's and not women's responsibility.

Fourth, by examining why policies of transformation were never advocated and how immigration policies have affected the nature and form of women's demands on the State in various historical periods, it is possible to ascertain how policies of inclusion have affected the women's movement's bargaining power in relation to the State. For policies of inclusion are merely remedial measures and their maintenance is dependent upon the will of the State. Currently, with the retraction of the Welfare State, many of the external support structures that these policies have created are being pulled out of the public sphere and placed back in the private sphere (for example health care and other caring services). By analyzing this process, it is possible to demonstrate how the women's movement is being affected in the present period, as well as to determine the impact this retraction will have on women belonging to different races and classes, most notably foreign domestic workers.

Fifth, by analyzing the issues in this multifaceted and multi-layered way, it is possible to examine how and why the State is able to enact policies that maintain intra-gender relations of sub-ordination and domination. A high demand for domestic workers is not enough for such a policy to function effectively. This policy also requires an abundant supply of women willing to work under increasingly restrictive conditions in the hopes of attaining Canadian citizenship. By examining the dynamics of the global stratification of labour that is characterized by gender, race and class, it is possible to ascertain how these dynamics are replayed within the microcosm of Canadian society. Moreover, it allows for an assessment of how State interests are served by enacting such policies.

Last, there are few documented case studies that provide an in-depth analysis based on the intersection of race, class and gender oppression. The issue of domestic workers in Canada provides a good case study (white mistress, non-white servant) in which the intersection of these variables can be delineated within a historical context. In addition, by assessing the connection between Canadian immigration policy with respect to domestic workers and the women's movement's demands for equality in the political and economic spheres, it is possible to connect State policies with women's demands. This, in turn, allows for a gendered, race and class perspective on Canadian immigration policy. Such a perspective is lacking in current immigration studies.

Consequently, the following work fills a gap in both existing immigration and socialist feminist literature.

Notes

1. Although feminists, such as Nancy Fraser, have raised the issue of multiple publics, this study, for reasons of parsimony, will use the more generic term of the public sphere.
2. Sedef Arat-Koc, "In the Privacy of Our Own Home: Foreign Domestic Workers as the Solution to the Crisis in the Domestic Sphere in Canada," *Studies in Political Economy* 28 (Spring 1989), 36. Although this phrase will be used repeatedly throughout the text, for reasons of simplicity, it will not be cited again.
3. *Ibid.*, 37.
4. For more on this analysis, see *ibid.*, 37–8
5. Analyses surrounding this issue have tended to analyze the issue in terms of race and class (i.e.: who benefits from domestic workers' labour) (Sedef Arat-Koc, "In the Privacy of Our Own Home: Foreign Domestic Workers as the Solution to the Crisis in the Domestic Sphere in Canada," *Studies in Political Economy* 28 (Spring 1989), 22–58); in terms of how some women function as agents of exploitation by acting as gatekeepers in foreign women of colour's quest to attain Canadian citizenship (Abigail Bakan and Daiva K. Stasiulis, "Making the Match: Domestic Placement Agencies and the Recialization of Women's Household Work," *Signs: Journal of Women in Culture and Society* 20.21 (Winter 1995), 303–335); in terms of how race and class operate as global systems of oppression which manifest themselves in policies regulating domestic workers' lives and working conditions (Ruth Lynette Harris, *The Transformation of Canadian Policies and Programs to Recruit Foreign Labour: The Case of Caribbean Female Domestic Workers, 1950's-1990's* (Ph.D. Dissertation: Michigan State University, 1988), Patricia Daenzer *Regulating Class Privilege: Immigrant Servants in Canada, 1940s-1990s* (Toronto: Canadian Scholars Press, 1993), Abigail Bakan and

Daiva K. Stasiulis, "Foreign Domestic Worker Policy in Canada and the Social Boundaries of Modern Citizenship," *Science and Society* 58.1 (Spring 1994), 7-33); in terms of racist immigration policies and their effects on women of colour originating from the third world (Agnes Calliste, "Canada's Immigration Policy and Domestics from the Caribbean: The Second Domestic Scheme," *Race, Class and Gender: Bonds and Barriers*, ed. Jesse Vorste (Toronto: Garamond Press, 1991), 136-169, Agnes Calliste, "Race, Gender and Canadian Immigration Policy: Blacks from the Caribbean, 1900-1932," *Journal of Canadian Studies* 28.4 (Winter 1993-94), 131-148, Vic Satzewich, "Racism and Canadian Immigration Policy: The Government's View of Caribbean Migration, 1962-1966," *Canadian Ethnic Studies* 21.1 (1989), 77-97) and in terms of how the women's movement is currently dealing with the issue (Rina Cohen, "A Brief History of Racism in Immigration Policies for Recruiting Domestics," *Canadian Woman Studies* 14.2 (1994), 83-86, Felicita O. Villasin and M. Ann Phillips, "Falling Through the Cracks: Domestic Workers and Progressive Movements," *Canadian Woman Studies* 14.2 (1994), 87-90).

6. Sedef Arat-Koc, "In the Privacy of Our Own Home: Foreign Domestic Workers as the Solution to the Crisis in the Domestic Sphere in Canada," *Studies in Political Economy* 28 (Spring 1989), 37.

7. For future reference within this text, when Linda Trimble is referred to or these periods are discussed, the references and discussion are based on pages 19-28 in her Ph.D. dissertation entitled *Coming Soon to a Station Near You: The Process and Impact of the Canadian Radio-Telecommunication Commission's Involvement in Sex-Role-Stereotyping* (Ph.D. Dissertation: Queen's University, 1990)..

8. Barbara Roberts, "'A Work of Empire': Canadian Reformers and British Female Immigration," *A Not Unreasonable Claim: Women and Reform in Canada, 1880s-1920s*, ed. Linda Kealey (Toronto: The Women's Press, 1979), 187.

9. Carol Bacchi, *Liberation Deferred? The Ideas of the English Canadian Suffragists, 1877-1918* (Canada: University of Toronto Press, 1983), 105-7, 113.

10. In this work, the term the women's movement refers only to the English–Canadian women's movement. This limitation is adhered to for two reasons. First, the Québec women's movement did not gain popular currency, both in numbers and in strength, until the 1960s.

Second, it has tended to direct its demands towards the Québec provincial government as opposed to the Canadian federal government. Thus, on both counts, it falls outside of the purview of this discussion.

11. Nancy Fraser, "Talking About Needs: Interpretive Contests as Political Conflicts in Welfare-State Societies," *Ethics* 99 (January 1989), 300.

12. Jane Errington, "Pioneers and Suffragists," *Changing Patterns: Women in Canada* eds. Sandra Burt, Lorraine Code and Lindsay Dorney (Toronto: McClelland & Stewart, 1990), 76.

13. This phrase is taken from the title of Sedef Arat-Koc's article "In the Privacy of Our Own Home: Foreign Domestic Workers as the Solution to the Crisis in the Domestic Sphere in Canada," *Studies in Political Economy* 28 (Spring 1989), 22-58. While this phrase will be used again in this text, for reasons of parsimony it will not be cited again.

14. See Vijay Agnew, "Canadian Feminism and Women of Color," *Women's Studies International Forum* 16 (1993), 217-227. Linda Briskin, "Identity Politics and the Hierarchy of Oppression," *Feminist Review* 35 (1990), 102-106. Zillah Eisenstein, *The Color of Gender: Reimagining Democracy* (USA: University of California Press, 1994). Marlee Kline, "Women's Oppression and Racism: Critique of the Feminist Standpoint," *Race, Class, Gender: Bonds and Barriers*, ed. Jesse Vorst (Toronto: Garamond Press, 1991), 39-55. Lynne Segal, *Is the Future Female? Troubled Thoughts on Contemporary Feminism* (London: Virago Press, 1987).

15. Melanie Randall, "Feminism and the State: Questions for Theory and Practice," *Resources for Feminist Research* 17 (1988), 12-3.

16. Mary Wollstencraft, *A Vindication of the Rights of Women* (USA: Penguin Books, 1992).

17. See Simone de Beauvoir, *The Second Sex* (New York: Bantam Books, 1969). Zillah Eisenstein, *The Radical Future of Liberal Feminism* (New York: Longmans, 1981). Sara Evans, "The Politics of Liberal Feminism," *Social Science Quarterly* 64 (1983), 880-897.

18. See Shulamith Firestone, *The Dialectic of Sex: The Case for Feminist Revolution* (New York: William Morrow, 1970). Marilyn French, *The War Against Women* (New York: Ballantine Books, 1992). Kate Millet, *Sexual Politics* (New York: Avon Books, 1970).

19. See Christine Delphy, *Close to Home: A Materialist Analysis of Women's Oppression* (Amherst: University of Massacheusetts Press, 1984). Susan

Gardiner, "Women's Domestic Labour" *New Left Review* 89 (1975), 47–58.
Maxine Molyneux, "Women in Socialist Societies: Problems of Theory and Practice," *Of Marriage and the Market: Women's Subordination in International Perspective*, eds. Chandra Talpade, Ann Russo and Lourdes Torres (USA: Indiana University Press, 1991), 51–80.

Chapter 1

SETTING THE STAGE
Women Belong to the Hearth and Home!

From the mid–nineteenth century until 1929, when women were formally granted the right to vote and gained legal recognition as persons, middle class white women engaged heavily in reform activities. The involvement of these women reformers in immigration, temperance, education, and child and female labour was often motivated by fears of social degeneration.[1] They wanted to ensure that Canada would remain a predominantly British, Anglo–Saxon nation, retaining the traditional family form based on a division of spheres as its foundation. Although women's reform activities expanded the scope of women's socially acceptable public participation and the range of employment available to women, they ultimately had the effect of reinforcing the notion that domestic labour was women's responsibility and the unpaid contribution that they should make to society. Their activities also buttressed the definition of who constituted a desirable citizen, while the race and class bias of their activities exacerbated divisions among women and structured domestic work. Black women, seen as undesirable citizens, were restricted to employment in domestic service where they were paid low wages, while British domestics, elevated in social and economic status, were free to pursue other employment.

Between 1840 and 1930, the Canadian economy developed along the lines of industrial capitalism while politics came to be governed by liberal democratic norms. As part of these new political and economic arrangements, the economy began to operate independently of the State. Lack of government regulation in the new capitalist system created a citizenry polarized by class and further divided along lines of sex and race; and although voting rights and other features of national citizenry were the objects of State legislation, the private sphere was decreed untouchable.[2] Traditionally, the State had regarded the family as residing outside the realm of legislative power, which meant that instead of empowering women to govern their own households, governing practices in the domestic sphere were left up to the male household heads.[3]

The State's specific construction of the public–private divide depended on particular assumptions about the public and the private domains. The domestic and the public spheres were categorized as irreconcilable, each belonging to a different gender.[4] Although the division of spheres was "...pronounced [as] 'natural' and therefore politically uncontestable..."[5], women's marginal position was, in fact, given legal strength by denying them access to educational institutions and the paid public sphere and withholding ownership rights from them.[6] Women were given a backhanded form of legal recognition, in the sense that they were made "...the objects of public policy long before they were officially recognized in law as legitimate political actors".[7] The State ordained that women, because they were so intrinsically linked with the private realm, had no place in the public sphere.[8]

The issue dividing the two spheres was gender. The private sphere was not only where women were thought to belong, but the values associated with this sphere – altruism, caring, devotion, and so on – came to define women's identity. As such, women were considered unequipped to participate in public sphere activities. The functioning of the family and the economy would be undermined by extending to women citizenship rights based on liberal democratic norms.[9] This was the result of deeply ingrained perceptions about citizenship and citizenship rights.

As Young (1989) has pointed out, citizenship and citizenship rights within liberal democracies are premised on the notion of a universal ideal. As such, they emphasize that all citizens have certain attributes in common, thereby assuming a certain degree of similarity among citizens. Moreover, the notion of a universal ideal means that laws and norms are blind to individual and group particularities and thus are equally applicable to all citizens of the State. Women, associated with and responsible for the domestic domain, came to be viewed as guardians of the physical, emotive, moral and spiritual realms, and consequently as possessing characteristics antithetical to those of the logical and orderly public sphere. Thus commonality among citizens could only be maintained by excluding women from citizenship and citizenship rights.[10] It was believed that granting women citizenship rights would destroy the carefully established "natural" order that was founded on a strict division of spheres.[11]

During this era, however, women were not entirely quiescent. In the 1870s some Canadian women began to organize in order to bring about changes in their status. Seeking to transform the inequitable gender relations upon which Canadian society was structured, these predominantly middle class professional women, called "equal rights feminists"[12], initiated the suffrage campaign. They based their arguments for female suffrage on the inherent equality of the sexes but did not limit their quest for equality to the vote: they envisioned far-reaching changes in the structure of Canadian society. Despite these women's outspoken and eloquent arguments for female enfranchisement, the suffrage movement did not gain widespread currency until "maternal feminists"[13] joined its ranks.

Maternal feminists, mostly white middle class women, accepted the existing gender and racial order. They were given a strong political voice because they sought to model the public sphere on that which was already viewed as the acceptable model in the private sphere.[14] These women came to support suffrage as a result of their social reform activities which were both race and class biased. These activities had a triple effect: they expanded the scope of white women's public participation;

they expanded, within the limited parameters of women's traditional role, the range of employement open to white women while increasing their access to education and employment; and they helped lay the legislative and institutional basis for the Welfare State which was to emerge in the 1930s. All of these, however, were premised on notions of women's traditional role in the home. Black Canadian women continued to be confined to jobs in domestic service where they worked for low wages. They occupied an inferior status to British domestics since they were unable to benefit from their formal legal rights to the same degree as their British counterparts and white female employers. Maternal feminists' goal was not sexual equality, but a strengthening of the Anglo–Saxon nation, the traditional family structure and women's established role within these institutions.

With their support, the nature and form of the suffrage movement changed. Women gained legal recognition and full citizenship rights, but the ideology of separate spheres was reinforced and women's subordinate status in the economic and social structures of Canadian society was entrenched. Women thus entered the political realm as "gendered citizens who embodied dominant impositional claims about the public/private divide and the appropriate gender order. It was by virtue of their womanhood, [their social reform activities] and their moral superiority and social consciousness, that they were recommended for citizenship rights."[15] Hence, the status quo prevailed once women attained citizenship rights. Maternal feminists' activities and ideology, informed by an acceptance of the existing class society that was ordered by gender and race, had the effect of ensuring that women remained responsible for domestic labour and that black women and lower class women would continue to provide a steady supply of this labour.

In order to explain this process, this chapter will first trace the rise of the ideology of separate spheres and the relationships that characterize it. Second, women's reform activities, focusing on immigration, temperance, education, and child and female labour will be examined. The suffrage movement – from the emergence of equal rights feminists and their ideology, activities, and limited popularity to their virtual eclipse from the public debate surrounding woman suffrage once maternal feminists joined the fray – will be examined against this backdrop. Maternal feminists' ascendancy within the suffrage movement had the effect of limited change for all women within the parameters of class and race bias. These same categories will be used to analyze women's status and activities in the public sphere after enfranchisement, with special reference to the Persons' Case of 1929.

I. The Dawning of a New Era: Industrialization, Urbanization, and the Rise of the Cult of True Womanhood

Between 1790 and the mid-nineteenth century, the separation between public and private spheres was not absolute.[16] Socially, politically and economically, the family was the basic unit, with family members working together in the struggle to survive in a rural and largely agricultural society. Women, especially married women, were required to obey men and had a lower status than men under the prevailing British law.[17] Despite this legal inequality and the sexual division of labour, some measure of sexual equality did exist. Because the family's survival depended on women's labour (work in the home, dairy and garden as well as reproduction) women's work was not deemed to be inherently less valuable than that of men; rather, it was recognized as contributing substantially to the family's material well-being.[18] The sexual division was not so rigid as to prevent women, if circumstances demanded it, from performing jobs traditionally defined as falling within the male preserve.[19]

Similarly, because the public-private divide was not firmly entrenched in either ideology or law, it was not unusual for women to participate in the political process on an equal footing with men outside the ruling elite. Colonial politics was hierarchically structured, with positions in the Legislative Assembly determined by male property owners who voted in members of the community's elite. Although the vote was not granted to men and women who were not property owners, these individuals could access the political process through petitions. Petitions were employed by individuals as a way of getting the law applied and by groups as a way of changing it. Age, class, ethnicity and religion did not prevent women from participating in this political process and their signatures carried the same weight as men's.[20]

It was only with the advent of male suffrage for those of European descent and the rise of party politics (1846–57) that participatory citizenship came to be defined by one's right to vote. Women, denied this right, continued to use the system of petitioning in order to influence important political issues of the day, such as temperance and prohibition.[21] It was the inefficiency of this mechanism that eventually led middle class white women to demand full citizenship in the form of suffrage.

By the mid–nineteenth century, the processes of industrialization and urbanization were well under way. Women and men began a process of migration that fundamentally transformed the Canadian landscape.[22] With the influx of new populations into urban areas and the rise of factory, mill and shop work, a class society was formed. Many of the functions that had traditionally been performed inside the home were transferred to the market economy. Both the rise of a class society and the decrease in domestic production had the effect of transforming the nature, form and function of the family.

The rise of a middle class was accompanied by a new ideology: the cult of true womanhood. This ideology, which permeated all classes, glorified women's role in the home, attempted to separate the public from the private sphere, and provided an ideal towards which the working class could aspire – that of having, or being, a stay–at–home wife who could direct all of her energies towards maintaining the family.[23] Women, perceived as the incarnation of values associated with the private sphere, such as caring, selflessness and morality, were idolized as the guardians of a shelter where men could escape a ruthless public sphere.[24] Many of women's traditional tasks (child bearing, child rearing and domestic work) did not move into the public sphere and thus were not remunerated. As a result, they and their work were viewed as inferior by a society that determined worth according to monetary reward.[25] This contradictory status mobilized middle class women to engage in reform activities throughout the second half of the nineteenth and early twentieth centuries.

For the working class, this ideal was largely unattainable given their material position. They worked in new areas of urban employment for low wages and under adverse conditions. An abundant supply of unskilled labourers and little State regulation left wages low, forcing women as well as men of this class to work in order to ensure their family's survival. Most working class women worked in factories. Others, who were unmarried and seeking a more genteel and respectable profession that they could leave upon marriage, worked in domestic service.[26] However, since many of the women working in domestic service tended to be black (both married and unmarried), this occupational category came to be governed by several racist assumptions.

Although the system of slavery in which "...black women, regardless of age, were the property and at the service of not only the white male slave owners, but also their wives, sons and daughters..."[27] had been abolished in 1833, it left a legacy of prescriptive stereotypes embedded in Canadian culture. Black women and men found themselves at the lower end of the socioeconomic hierarchy. Black women, both married and unmarried, were forced to work since a black male wage was insufficient to support a family.[28] Yet they were not able to enter any occupation other than domestic service because "...regardless of who you were and how educated you were... even if the employer would employ you, those that you had to work with would not work with you."[29] Black women were thus perceived as doubly suitable for domestic work, because they were women and because they were black; and, unlike white women in this occupation, they were expected to remain in service for the duration of their working career while being paid less than their white counterparts. Such attitudes towards skin colour fuelled the development of an intra-occupational hierarchy based on race. These prescriptive and structural elements congealed into a racism that provided the ideological framework within which reform women's activities regarding domestic work would be structured.

By the 1880s, the divisions among Canadian women paralleled the class and race divisions of the new urban and industrial society. Yet Canadian law[30] and ideology ensured that all women occupied an inferior social and economic status. There were fewer opportunities for single and married women to work in the paid workforce. Society expected women to stay in the private domain and tend to their family's needs. White middle class women with some skills or training who did not marry, and thus were unable to remain in the private sphere, were expected to engage in professions that were logical out-growths of woman's traditional roles, such as "teaching, nursing, and domestic service."[31] Both women and broader society perceived this work as temporary, expecting it to end once women entered the sanctity of matrimony.[32] A small group of women who were dissatisfied with the conditions that governed women's experience and who wanted to expand women's access to the public sphere began to mobilize in support of female suffrage. These women were the equal rights feminists.

At the same time, Canada's nation-building endeavors seemed to be hindered by a number of social problems resulting from urbanization and industrialization. The disparity between the ideology glorifying middle class women's status and the actual status of these women, combined with a rise in their leisure time due to a decrease in time-consuming domestic tasks, led many middle class women to engage in reform activities.[33] Active in the areas of immigration, temperance, education, and child and female labour laws, these women mobilized for female suffrage once they saw it as a means of achieving their reforms. Known as maternal feminists, they came to dominate the suffrage movement.

II. The Reform Movement: Ladies as Bastions of the 'New' Social Order

In the 1880s, middle class women began to step outside the private sphere and engage in social causes. These women forsook the role of ladies of leisure in order to attempt to impose order in the public sphere. They believed that the processes of urbanization and industrialization were causing a great deal of problems in the form of increased numbers of foreigners. During these years, the fertility rate of the Protestant population was declining.[34] Canadian society was no longer overwhelmingly composed of Anglo-Saxons. Two and a half million Southern and Eastern Europeans came to Canada in the two decades prior to World War One. They settled into crowded areas of already congested cities.[35] Reformers[36] viewed their influx as detrimental to the development of Canadian society in a number of ways. Not only did their presence undermine the British Anglo-Saxon character of the fledgling Nation-State but the newcomers engaged in a number of activities, such as drinking, that challenged the middle class morality, values and social structure that the reformers wished to preserve. In fact, motivated by race and class concerns, these women actively sought to increase the British component of the population through the recruitment and immigration of domestic workers. This reform activity was undertaken with the goal of attaining racial purity.[37]

Reformers believed that the dwindling proportion of Anglo-Saxons within Canadian society was the result of decreasing numbers of Anglo-Saxon women who were giving birth, in combination with a growing non-English population.[38] These women sought to increase the Anglo-Saxon component by encouraging women's emigration from Britain. As Mrs. F. H. Torrington, the president of the National Council of Women in Canada, stated in

1913, "Keep back the foreigner. Give us good, sound British stock – women already British, already civilized, already subjected to both earth and heaven for conduct."[39] Although they believed that it was possible to assimilate foreigners, with the exception of blacks and Asians, these women sought to ensure that the Anglo–Saxon component of the nation would remain dominant.[40] Working towards this goal, a network of women's organizations, both in Britain and Canada, screened and selected women for emigration to Canada. These British women were slated to work in domestic service with the hope that they would become future mothers of the nation.[41] Reformers' work in this area enabled many British women to eventually become employers of servants themselves.[42]

The 1880s heralded women's increased involvement in immigration. While the British Women's Emigration Agency selected and sent the women from Britain, Canadian women reformers and volunteer groups played the crucial role of assuming guardianship of the women once they landed in Canada.[43] In 1884, Ellen Joyce of the British Women's Emigration Agency was sent to Canada in order to participate in talks with Canadian reformers and federal immigration officials concerning the inadequacy of the current system. This agency's mandate was fulfilled, and a more stringent system that made provisions for specific administrative processes was instituted. It was decided that the process of selecting the women, based on specific criteria, would continue to be carried out in Britain. Candidates were examined to make sure that they possessed high moral standards and had a respectable background. They were also required to demonstrate certain occupationally–useful qualities, including a positive attitude, a high level of intelligence and peak physical condition.[44] Middle class British women belonging to a network of interrelated organizations rendered a decision once they had assessed all the relevant information. They then forwarded the files to Canadian federal immigration officers and reformers. Access to these files – and thus to more specific information about these women – often made it possible to place them in suitable domestic positions before they even landed in Canada.[45]

Temporary shelters or hostels, such as the YWCA or Homes of Welcome, provided an interim refuge for the women once they set foot on Canadian soil. Women reformers ran these facilities with the aim of keeping the newcomers under a watchful eye. The reasoning behind such strict control was that, if guarded, female immigrants would not stray from the high level of morality expected from future mothers of the nation. Many of these women reformers wanted greater government support as a way of enhancing their power and boosting their funding. The efficient and effective functioning of their immigration activities was dependent upon these resources.[46]

Beginning in 1906, the federal government began to make financial contributions to some of the women's temporary shelters and hostels. After 1910, Travelers' Aid assumed part of the responsibility for bringing in domestic servants, thereby marking the beginning of institutionalization. Representatives of Traveler's Aid, responsible for all unsupervised women once they landed in Canada, were charged with sending the women to an authorized hostel or lodging.[47] In 1919, the Canadian Council of Immigration for Women for Household Service was established to oversee the influx of female domestic servants. The council was composed of representatives of provincial governments, the various hostels, the Women's Christian Temperance Union, the YWCA, the churches, the Girls' Friendly Society, Business Girls' Clubs, the National Council of Women in Canada, the Imperial Order of the Daughters of the Empire, the Women's Institutes, and the Patriotic League – all of whom were involved in the importation of female domestics. The enactment of the Empire Settlement Act of 1922, designed in part to shift the surplus of educated middle class females in Britain to Canada, signalled the end of reformers' control over female immigration. Henceforth, it was to be controlled by the government.[48]

The British Women's Emigration Agency and the reform women were responsible for bringing 8 500 British women into Canada between the years 1884 and 1914.[49] Most of the women went into domestic service with the understanding that they would work in their assigned position in return for their paid passage. Yet many of them quickly escaped the private sphere to work in public service industry jobs, in hotels and restaurants for example, where the rate of remuneration was better.[50] Once World War One began, fewer British women were willing to travel to Canada to work as domestics. The lure of new employment increasingly available to women in Britain in areas associated with war work and white collar work, such as clerical and sales work, was infinitely more attractive to these women than travelling overseas to work in private homes. These occupations were better remunerated, had well-defined hours, and did not require travelling to a foreign country.[51] Despite the scarcity of women who were willing to emigrate to Canada in order to engage in domestic work, the rules and regulations defining immigration were already racially structured and well-entrenched.

Between 1845 and 1924, Canada had an open door immigration policy. However, Asians and blacks were excluded from this policy. Individuals and groups were often evaluated subjectively according to the applicant's moral, economic and social status. Those deemed undesirable could be denied entry under the Immigration Acts of 1906 and 1910. The government also had the power to deport workers already in the country. After 1910, the decision of whether or not to grant an individual entry was based, to a considerable extent, on their race.[52] Generally, government officials rejected Caribbean applicants who met every immigration requirement,[53] asserting that they would eventually become a drain on public funds.[54] These judgments were based on racial stereotypes that predominated within the collective Canadian ideological frame of reference. It was believed that individuals with dark skin were mentally, morally, physically and socially inferior to whites and that their presence in Canada would most likely result in a host of social and economic problems.[55]

As Satzewich (1989) has noted, three racist beliefs underpinned Canadian immigration policy. First, it was assumed that people with coloured skin, being generally from warmer climates, would be physically unable to adjust to the harsh Canadian winters.

They were thus likely to suffer from poor health, work less efficiently than whites, and become social liabilities. It was also assumed that, "...because of their biology, they were unable to change culturally and unable to adjust to a capitalist and competitive Canadian society."[56] Last, it was believed that their presence would cause racial strife in Canada. This "racialized" immigration policy reflects the perception that only whites could fit into many Canadians' preconceived notions of what constituted a proper citizenry.[57]

Prior to 1909, Nova Scotian employers who visited the Caribbean recruited local women to work as domestics in Canada. These women were viewed as an inexpensive and abundant source of labour. While white European women often left domestic service as soon as jobs in the public sector became available, black women, unable to avail themselves of jobs in the public sector, were forced to remain in domestic service, working for lower wages than those offered to their white counterparts.[58]

The desire to increase this supply of labour led some Canadian women to place pressure on the State to admit these women to Canada as domestic servants. This pressure resulted in the development of the first Caribbean Domestic Scheme of 1910–11. J. M. Authier, a former American consul, recruited one hundred Guadeloupean women to work for Québec's middle class. They were expected to work for five dollars a month for a period of two years in exchange for their eighty dollar fare to Canada, while white servants in similar positions were paid twelve to fifteen dollars a month.[59] Not only did the racist ideology underpinning Canadian society and structuring the Canadian labour force justify the lower wages paid to black women, but the Caribbean's colonial status which was associated with underdevelopment and its history of slavery also contributed.[60]

The Immigration Branch adopted a policy that limited black immigration in 1911. This policy was implemented as a result of the imminent arrival of two larger groups of Guadeloupean women. Caribbean women were considered dependent liabilities to Canadian society[61], while British servants were seen as prospective wives and mothers who would help build and strengthen the idealized Anglo–Saxon nation. As such, Caribbean women were not granted the same rights as their British counterparts and were subject to the constant threat of deportation. The scheme to import the Guadeloupean women was subsequently terminated under the pretext that these women lacked the requisite physical and moral characteristics.[62] During the economic recession of 1913–15, ninety–one domestics who were laid off and were unable to find jobs – because white women were more willing to work in this occupation – were sent back to the Caribbean. This high rate of deportation became an argument in favor of refusing Caribbean blacks, especially women, entry into Canada.[63] In 1922, the same year that Canadian immigration officials actively sought to attract British women, Order–in–Council P.C. 717[64] removed black Caribbeans' right to immigrate to Canada. Only domestic servants who could prove that they already had employment in Canada were exempted from this law. Black Caribbeans, however, were treated differently than their white counterparts. They did not receive the same social services provided to British domestics by immigration societies.[65]

Canadian women's reform activities in the area of immigration thus had the effect of structuring immigration rules and regulations in accordance with the racist ideology to which they subscribed. Viewed as unassimilable, blacks were largely denied entry into Canada. Slavery, although abolished in 1833, left a long–standing legacy in Canadians' collective frame of reference. As a result, black Caribbeans who were lucky enough to be accepted into the nation's fold were still relegated to menial jobs in white middle class homes. Between 1927 and 1931, of the four hundred and ninety–nine black Caribbean immigrants who entered Canada, seventy–eight percent worked in domestic service.[66] The Immigration Superintendent's statement in 1918 that "Colored labour is not generally speaking in demand in Canada and it is not only regarded as the lowest grade but it is the last to be taken on and the first to be discharged in most enterprises"[67] exemplifies the economic, political and ideological realities that underpinned Canada's discriminatory immigration policies regarding domestic workers, policies that had been crafted to a large degree by women reformers.

Immigration was not the only area of reform activity geared towards maintaining racial purity. As Bacchi (1983) has demonstrated, the desire to maintain racial purity was part of a larger pattern, providing the ideological framework within which these women's reform activities in the areas of temperance, education, child and female labour were conducted. According to these women reformers, the decline of those of Anglo–Saxon extraction presented a threat to the emerging Canadian Nation–State. Consequently, they geared their activities towards increasing the size of the British population while attempting to assimilate and convert to Christianity all non–British immigrants. Their goal was to create a homogenous "white bred" society with uniform values. These values were to be based on the traditional allocation of sex roles with the family functioning as the most basic building–block of Canadian society.[68]

Although these women reformers altered the nature of the public–private divide by engaging in activities outside the home, in no way did they challenge the idea that their maternal role was their defining characteristic. They claimed that it was because they were mothers that they were obligated to protect their individual homes as well as the nation, which in effect was an extension of the home.[69] Through their reform activities they attempted to institutionalize these maternal values via legislation such as prohibition. They also worked towards creating new social institutions, such as schools, that would replace the family if it failed to operate according to the moral directives they had established as the prevailing ideal.[70] In addition, they advocated greater State intervention in areas that the Laissez–Faire State deemed to reside outside the purview of State power, such as factory legislation and Mothers' Pensions, in order to attain their goal. All of these activities provided the springboard for their involvement in the suffrage movement.

Reform women overwhelmingly focused on the issue of temperance, and it was this activity that converted the largest number of supporters to the cause of suffrage.[71] The Women's Christian Temperance Union was established as a tool to combat overzealous drinking. In 1883, it became a national organization. Women involved in this reform activity were worried that men who drank would inflict damage on society. They wanted to protect wives, mothers and children from those periodically under the influence and to protect homes from the detrimental effects of alcohol. These reformers viewed excessive drinking as an impediment to the new and greater society that they envisioned, and they associated this deviant behavior with foreigners and the working and upper classes.[72] The Women's Christian Temperance Union recruited many women by stressing their maternal role as guardians of the home and family. Their goal was to ward off evil from their homes and those of the community; an assault on individual families was equated with an assault on the Anglo-Saxon nation.[73]

Given that the State licensed the liquor trade, the women could only attain prohibition by changing State legislation. Consequently, the Women's Christian Temperance Union used the petition in order to introduce plebiscites on the issue. When referendums were held, however, the women's initiatives were repeatedly defeated by male voters.[74] Temperance Union women quickly realized their political impotence and became convinced that the sole route to success lay in attaining the vote. By 1891 each provincial branch had established a specific department to work towards attaining the vote.[75]

By the turn of the century, there was a Women's Christian Temperance Union in each of the provinces and the organization had a total of 10 000 members.[76] In 1906, realizing that the movement could not triumph unless women possessed the vote, the organization decided to focus all of its attention on women's suffrage. These women did not see the vote as a goal in itself, but the means by which a greater goal could be achieved – that of creating a reliable working class and society imbued with proper (middle class Anglo-Saxon) values and morality.[77] Because the Women's Christian Temperance Union endorsed the dominant social outlook, including the prevailing belief that women's proper role was that of wife and mother, many temperance men became suffragists and enlisted in suffrage societies.[78] This new support base would dilute the strength of equal rights feminists and change the tone of the suffrage campaign in a more conservative direction.

The Women's Christian Temperance Union, in conjunction with many other women's organizations devoted to social reform, fought for educational reforms. Reformers wanted the State to legislate compulsory education and sought to increase the educational opportunities available to women.[79] The Church came to support these reforms. Women's education was perceived as a back-up plan for those women who failed to adopt the prevailing model of the feminine ideal. Women who eschewed marriage would have the training to be self-sufficient, while compulsory education would Canadianize the new immigrant, instilling morality into girls who would one day instruct their own children.[80] Although both the reformers and the Church advocated increasing girls' education opportunities, their vision of reform was quite limited. They merely wanted to give girls the skills, through domestic science courses, that would help them in their future careers as mothers.[81]

As Bacchi (1983) has noted, the benefits envisioned were threefold. First, women would be able to use their new skills to make their husbands more comfortable at home, thereby preventing them from becoming philanderers and bar-hounds. Stable and sober families implied a strong, healthy workforce, and by extension a powerful nation. Second, women's knowledge of health issues would increase the nation's standard of living. Finally, by turning housework and child care into a profession that was governed by scientific principles, domestic labour's status would be enhanced and fewer women would look outside the home for personal gratification.[82]

Between 1893 and 1908 domestic science courses, early versions of home economics, were introduced into the public schools of thirty-two Canadian cities.[83] During these years, the number of women willing to work as domestics fell far below the level of demand. Although middle class reform women subscribed to the cult of true womanhood, it appears as if few wanted to clean their own homes.[84] By entrenching domestic science courses in the curriculum of Canada's public schools, middle class women served their own interests. An increased number of domestic workers was assured by restricting socially acceptable female employment to domestic work. This made it easier for middle class women to ensure the proper functioning of their homes while still having the leisure time to participate in public sphere activities, where they could act as guardians of their race. This reform was effected with a class bias and an awareness of class interests.[85] As the National Council of Women in Canada argued in 1898,

> It would be quite equal in mental development, and infinitely more useful, for a girl to learn the chemistry of food and its relation to the body, the science of ventilation, cleanliness, cookery and needlework, than to wear out brain tissue in puzzling out a lot of abstract questions, which will neither awaken the intelligence nor interest of the pupil... One of the great avenues of labour for which there is an unfailing demand is that of domestic help in the home...What we need in Canada to-day is skilled labour, and in order to secure greater opportunities for girls to acquire skill in the various womanly pursuits, an effort must be made to secure for them special technical education.[86]

Since immigration regulations did not permit black women to enter Canada, and since British and black Canadian women could not fill the demand for domestic labour, white middle class women were required to find a new supply of women willing to perform this work in Canada – these could only be white working class women.

Some of these women's reform organizations also supported higher education for women. However, as Bacchi (1983) has pointed out, there was a class component to this demand as well, since only middle class white women could afford to attend institutions of higher learning. These same women's organizations believed that only those women with a certain amount of education and intelligence should be allowed the vote, thus limiting suffrage to their own privileged race and class.[87] Moreover, because they believed that women should have higher education only in order to better enable them to carry out their role as guardians of the home, they did not mobilize in favour of more accessible professional employment for women. Hence, women who managed to obtain a professional education were only able to work in areas that were perceived as logical outgrowths of women's customary role as caregiver.

Their demands for increased access to higher education did not expand the range of occupations open to women; they did, however, reinforce a feminized role for women in the public sphere, a role that would continue to be ordered by race and class and which would ensure that women continued to be paid less than men. By framing its demands within the ideology of the cult of domesticity, the reform movement helped to solidify the ideological and material conditions that would structure women's subordinate economic situation for future generations.

This pattern was repeated in the reformers' efforts to effect changes in female and child labour. Allied with the capitalist class, these women took a strong stance against granting workers some measure of protection through the right to strike and to unionize. The type of legislative reforms that they advocated were merely designed to protect factory workers from the most obvious problems in the existing industrial system. Wanting to protect women from the worst effects of factory work in order to ensure the health of the Anglo-Saxon race, they advocated, among other things, the outlawing of child labour, with the belief that it was reducing the numbers of their race.[88] Yet they did not question the sexual hierarchy of the workplace, a hierarchy that working class women saw as integral to the elevation of their status.[89] This class bias reinforced divisions among women and limited the size of the suffrage movement.

Other reform activities, motivated by fears of race degeneration, were also geared toward strengthening the family. All had the consequence of entrenching the ideology of separate spheres and of limiting the development of new jobs for women to extensions of their traditional roles. As Bacchi (1983) highlights, women reformers did not believe that the family could be relied upon to indoctrinate children with the proper middle-class Anglo-Saxon morality. Therefore, in conjunction with other dominant groups (business and professional), they advocated instituting a secondary mechanism to accomplish this goal. Public schools, established in response to compulsory education, were to take over the socialization of children. Thus, new vocational opportunities were created for women[90] which, rather than detracting from women's natural function, merely professionalized it.

Most reformers restricted their campaigns for further State intervention to ones that would enforce women's role in the home. For example, demands for child welfare schemes and Mother's Pensions were premised on the belief that the State should provide for women who were unable to provide adequately for themselves and their children.[91] These programs had a dual effect. They reinforced the notion that children were women's responsibility and that women were needed at home for society to function properly. Other reform programs which ostensibly belonged to the province of motherhood, such as "...civic cleanliness, the city beautiful, education, civic morality, the protection of children from immoral influences, the reform of delinquent children, child labour, infant mortality, food adulteration, and public health,"[92] established women's role in politics, which was that of dealing with "women's issues".

Moreover, the maternal feminist and racist ideology that underpinned the reformers' agenda helped to entrench the acceptability of a class system organized along lines of gender and race. Through their activities, women reformers inadvertently structured women's subordinate economic status and circumscribed the range of activities available to women along the lines of traditional stereotypes about women's characteristics and roles. Women's nurturing function was established as natural and desirable, the notion of domestic work as a woman's preserve was entrenched in the ideological framework of the nation, and the racist ideology that designated some women as lesser in worth and more suitable for domestic service was entrenched in both the public and the private economic structures of the nation.

Consequently, while these middle class white women were accumulating power for themselves as the conscience of Canadian society, their activities had the effect of restricting the number of social and economic options available to other Canadian women.[93] The ideology to which they subscribed aimed at moderating the pace of change. Reform women determinedly argued against any change in the traditional family and social structure and actively geared their reforms towards maintaining it.[94] Hence, perceiving equal rights feminists as potential disrupters of the social order, reform women opposed the equality-seeking reforms that they had advanced in the late nineteenth century. Maternal feminists' opposition to equal rights feminists' demands for suffrage lasted until the early twentieth century, at which point, the strength of the reformers' ideology and their antagonism towards equal rights proposals led them to join the suffrage movement. Although the alliance was a strategic one, the reformers managed to infuse the movement with the ideology of maternal feminism and complete the process of limiting the possibility for change in women's status.

III. The Suffrage Movement: 1877-1918

In 1877, Emily Stowe, the first Canadian woman doctor, established the Toronto Women's Literary Society which changed its name in 1883 to the Canadian Woman Suffrage Association and became the first national organization to advocate female suffrage.[95] Stowe's belief in equal rights for women was a continuation of a Canadian feminist tradition.[96] It came to inform the ideology to which a small clique of women adhered and the basis on which they fought for suffrage. These women believed in women's right to classical, mathematical and scientific education. They believed that professional training and employment should be accessible to women, and that women should be able to pursue any type of employment they desired on an equal footing with men.[97]

In the main, the women who adhered to this position were professionals. They were a small group of women who had attempted to gain access to the public sphere in professions such as law, medicine, journalism and university teaching, and in doing so had come across blatant sexual discrimination. Those who were able to overcome the sex barrier were faced with lower paychecks. Most were ghettoized in areas associated with women's traditional caring functions that ensured their subordinate status.[98]

Between 1884 and 1889, the suffrage movement was largely unsuccessful given its limited support base. In 1889, Stowe and her daughter, Augusta Stowe-Gullen, inaugurated the Dominion Women's Enfranchisement Association, which soon founded branch societies in communities across the country. This expansion was possible as a result of improvements in communications (telephones) and transportation (trams). During the 1890s, many male and female reformers joined suffrage societies, and many of the reform associations, such as the Women's Christian Temperance Union, established suffrage branches devoted solely to obtaining female suffrage.[99]

Suffrage societies sprouted up across the country, yet support was largely limited to those middle class women who had entered new professions and occupations, such as sales and clerical work, and who were self-supporting.[100] Working class women did not have the time to engage in suffrage activities and the suffrage societies had neither the political nor the "woman" power to mobilize them.[101] While the former group of professionals believed that their subordinate status was the result of sexual discrimination, working class women did not adhere to this view. Most of them merely wanted to escape the toil of factory work and enter the private sphere of the home.[102]

Despite some reformers' conversion to woman suffrage, the

movement was not riding on a groundswell of support; in fact, the situation was the exact opposite.[103] The National Council of Women in Canada, inaugurated by Lady Ishbel Aberdeen in 1893, was founded on the belief that,

> Nature has assigned to us all our duties in life. To the man has been given the task of supporting the woman, of sustaining the home, of fighting the battles and of governing the family, the clan or the nation. To woman has been committed the charge of the home and the duty of exercising a moderating influence over all its occupants. The Suffragettes...are at war with nature. They want the women to be too much like men.[104]

This organization was devoted to preserving and furthering the middle class ideology of the cult of true womanhood and thus engaged in a number of reform activities with the goal of preserving the family unit as the basic building-block of the nation. As such, the organization emphatically dissociated itself from the vision that equal rights feminists espoused and repeatedly defeated suffrage resolutions passed by the Dominion Women's Enfranchisement Association and Canadian Suffrage Association in 1898, 1906, and 1907.[105]

In 1906 the Dominion Women's Enfranchisement Association adopted the new title of the Canadian Suffrage Association. Augusta Stowe-Gullen[106], Flora MacDonald Denison, and Margaret Blair Gordon headed this new organization. Although all three adhered to Stowe's feminist beliefs, Flora MacDonald Denison was the most outspoken proponent of equal rights feminism. She did not subscribe to the view that giving women the vote would translate into a greater degree of civic morality, nor did she believe that women could only contribute to society by adopting the role associated with "social housekeeping". She advocated no-fault divorce, birth control, and believed that women should be economically independent, even after marriage, as it was the only way in which they could avoid being forced to remain dependent upon men.[107] In effect, by stressing the idea that women should have the right to define themselves as autonomous and by equating women's rights with human rights, she posed a challenge to the very structure of the Canadian family, the bedrock upon which Canadian society was seen to rest.

Despite the exposure that these views gained within broader society and the expansion of Canadian Suffrage Association affiliates in Saint John, Victoria, Winnipeg and Montreal, equal rights feminists remained an ideological and numerical minority within the suffrage movement. They had little power outside of Toronto.[108] It was only with the National Council of Women in Canada's endorsement of suffrage in 1910[109] that women's suffrage gained widespread support the participation of educated house-wives was on the rise. By that time, the suffrage movement was largely dominated by middle class reform men and women who espoused the ideology of maternal feminism which did not threaten the prevailing social structure but instead emphasized women's special nurturing and maternal qualities.[110] As Nellie McClung eloquently stated:

> If politics are corrupt, it is all the more reason that a new element should be introduced. Women will I believe supply that new element, that puri-fying influence. Men and women were intended to work together, and will work more ideally together, than apart, and just as the mother's influence as well as the father's is needed in the bringing up of children and in the affairs of the home, so are they needed in the larger home, the state.[111]

With the National Council of Women in Canada's endorsement of suffrage the movement lost all connection to women's equal rights, and some of the equal rights feminists even began to profess maternal feminist arguments in order to advance the cause of suffrage.[112]

After 1910, the Canadian Suffrage Association and the National Council of Women in Canada cooperated in an uneasy alliance, but the Council women were, most often, the dominant force when the groups presented themselves in public. In 1914, the National Council women and their supporters attempted to wrest control of the Canadian Suffrage Association.[113] They were quickly forced out of the organization but managed to found the National Equal Franchise Union which attracted the support of many housewives who did not wish to challenge the traditional family structure.[114] By that time, however, the Canadian Suffrage Association, as an organization, largely accepted and advanced maternal feminist arguments for suffrage.[115] In effect, maternal feminists countered the potential of equal rights feminism by associating women's political role with that of the moral conscience of the nation and social reform. Women were to become the guardians of the Anglo-Saxon race: they would reinstate middle class values and norms in order to ensure a society that functioned smoothly and properly according to a strict division of spheres. Canadians of British extraction would retain their dominant position as long as the family remained a cornerstone of society. This could be done by granting the vote to women who would obey their husbands' directives.[116]

Many of the suffragists who adhered to maternal feminist arguments, including Nellie McClung, did not want the vote granted to all women; they merely wanted married women and women of British descent to possess the vote.[117] This was to be accomplished by means of an intelligence or educational qualification. It would off-set non-Anglo-Saxon foreigners' influence in the political arena since many of them did not possess the requisite educational certificate.[118] As Mrs. Gordon Grant stated in 1888, in an address to the Women's Christian Temperance Union:

> even the foreigner, who perhaps can neither read nor write, but who by residing on Canadian soil one year and taking the oath of allegiance, though he may know nothing of our laws, nothing of the men who aspire to office, perhaps he cannot speak one word of English, and yet he can say, who shall be our legislators, while we

women are placed side by side with idiots,
lunatics, and children...Shall she have no voice as
to what sort of laws shall govern her children and
demand their obedience, while a man too igno-
rant to read, and therefore incapable of forming
an intelligent opinion, has the legal right to assist
in forming our laws by his vote.[119]

An educationally restricted franchise would increase the weight
of the middle class family vote and hence that which represented
the reformers' values.[120] Maternal feminists were thus racially
and class motivated – they wanted the vote in order to boost the
power that members of their race and class already possessed.
They also wanted the vote in order to legislate their social
reforms thereby ensuring a stable and sober working class that
would bolster their own economic position.[121]

As Strong-Boag (1991) has pointed out, many of these women,
viewing the existing organization of party politics as detrimen-
tally affecting the evolution of the race, wished to transform it.
They envisioned a system in which well-educated Anglo-Saxon
middle class women, immune to political conflict, would act as
impartial judges on issues of public importance. In effect, they
would have ultimate control when making decisions that affected
the Nation-State. This role was justified by stating that because
middle class women possessed a higher level of morality they
should be guardians of the nation.[122] By countering the opposition's anti-suffrage arguments that were premised on the notion
that women are too good to vote with ones that stated that it was
precisely middle class women's morality that entitled them to
vote[123], maternal feminists reinforced both the notion of the
sexes' different natures and the divisions that already existed
within the ranks of women.

The lack of efforts made by maternal feminists to recruit
working class women into their associations, and the disdainful
treatment that was meted out to the few who dared to attend
their meetings fomented hostility among working class women.
The class biased platform did little to counter working women's

belief that the suffragists wanted them to conform to their middle class standards.[124] For working class women, it was not the vote that was essential but the protective legislation that they could effect once they possessed the vote. Hence, working class women allied themselves with the men of their class. They organized within established labour groups and created the Women's Labour League in order to win the vote, an essential tool for attaining pay equity, which would in turn improve their and their family's material status.[125]

Farm women from the Prairie provinces found themselves in a similar position, allying themselves with the men of their class. Farm men, fearing the disproportionate influence of the urban sector and wanting to increase their vote, mobilized with farm women for woman suffrage through the Grain Growers of Manitoba and Saskatchewan and the United Farmers of Alberta.[126] These women attributed their oppression to economic factors. They wanted the vote to increase the political weight of the agrarian sector, and thus were unwilling to side with the suffrage ladies of leisure to whom they attributed, in part, their peripheral status.[127]

Although both of these groups of women advanced different arguments for woman suffrage, by the time they had begun to mobilize, maternal feminism had become the dominant discourse informing women's roles and rights. Once the war began, the maternal feminists placed the war effort above the cause of suffrage.[128] Due to the exigencies of war, the economy was fully mobilized in 1916. In order to fill the demand for wartime employees, many white women entered the new industrial areas associated with war work. The government was behind this effort to mobilize women to enter the workforce, but women's new roles were seen as a temporary measure resulting from an emergency situation. It was fully expected that women would return to the home and resume their maternal duties after the war.[129] In the end, women were not granted the right to vote out of a belief in the equality of the sexes. Rather, it was granted as a reward for their service during wartime.[130]

The three Prairie provinces enfranchised women in 1916, and

because the 1898 Franchise Law stated that federal electoral lists were to be drawn from provincial ones, the federal government was required to consider the issue of female suffrage. Ontario and British Columbia followed suit in 1917. That same year, Prime Minister Borden legislated the Wartime Elections Act giving the nearest female family member of enlisted men the vote and promising to enfranchise all other women of British or Canadian citizenship over the age of twenty-one within a year. This was accomplished in 1918. Women in Nova Scotia received the provincial vote in the same year but those in New Brunswick, Prince Edward Island and Québec had to wait until 1919, 1922, and 1940 respectively.[131]

Because the granting of woman suffrage was touted by male politicians as a reward for women's selfless war effort and because of maternal feminism's ideological power, woman suffrage lost any connection to the notion of equal rights. Yet despite maternal feminism's ideal of creating a new society and a political structure free from immorality, change was essentially negligible. Women's traditional stance of non-partisanship meant that those who entered the political arena found themselves marginalized by the very structures they had wanted to abolish or, at a minimum, stand above.[132] Maternal feminism's ascendancy meant that most women did not actively try to access the political arena, and those who did, such as Agnes McPhail, were viewed as freaks.

Moreover, the reinforcement of race and class divisions among women meant that mobilization along gender lines was virtually impossible. The Woman's Party, formed in 1918 by Constance Hamilton of the National Equal Franchise Union, was a failure, lasting only two months and viewed by most non-middle class and non-white women as an "...urban, elitist and a conservative... group"[133] geared toward maintaining the status quo.

IV. Women Are People Too:
The Persons' Case of 1929

Between 1919 and 1929, the suffrage movement did remain committed to the cause of establishing women's legal person-hood. Under the prevailing British law, women were not legally recognized as persons and so were unable to serve in the Senate. In 1919, many women's organizations[134] passed resolutions urging the Canadian government to appoint a woman to the Senate. The Conservative federal government, refusing to accom-modate the women by pointing to the existing constitutional definition of the term persons, frustrated white middle class women's attempts to gain some measure of representation for their sex, class, and race.[135]

In 1927, Edmonton police magistrate Emily Murphy learned of a seldom used section of the Supreme Court Act whereby parties with vested interests could request a new constitutional reading of sections under the British North America (BNA) Act. On October 19, 1927, Emily Murphy, Nellie McClung, Henrietta Muir Edwards, Irene Palbry, and Louise McKinney lobbied the Supreme Court of Canada to have their case heard. On April 24, 1928, the verdict rendered stated that women were indeed "...not 'qualified persons' within the meaning of Section 24 of the BNA Act, 1867, and therefore...not eligible for appointment by the governor general to the Senate of Canada."[136] These women took the case to the Judicial Committee of the Privy Council in England and, on October 18, 1929 this body announced that they were henceforth to be treated as persons in the legal sense.[137] Despite this legal gain, which completed the process of granting women the formal trappings of citizenship, women's status remained one of subordination, further layered by the race and class to which they belonged.

The race, class, professional, geographic, urban/rural divisions among women limited equal rights feminists' earlier ambition of a united and collectively liberated womanhood.[138] Although society generally accepted that working class and single women were needed to work in the public sphere, and although they continued to enter new white collar occupations, they continued to be paid less than men while being shunted into subordinate positions. This was the result of the widespread belief that women's work in the public sphere was only transient and would end once women got married.[139] While women continued to enter the teaching, nursing and clerical professions at a growing rate, few women were able to access the prestigious legal and medical professions.[140]

Ultimately, maternal feminism became a dominant discourse guiding the structure of Canadian society and the type of policies that the State would effect regarding women in the future. Although women were granted the vote and recognized as persons in the eyes of the law, they found themselves palpably removed from the very governmental structures that they had sought to reform. Middle class women continued to remain outside the public sphere, often attending to their new "profession" of motherhood. Few women were candidates in elections and even fewer held elected posts. Simultaneously, most suffrage societies lost their visionary character and faded into the woodwork, with the vote becoming merely a public means to display their maternal qualities.[141] Women's political participation continued to be arrested by pre-existing impediments that remained in place.

V. Maternal Feminism's Legacy: Status Ascription by Race, Class and Gender

Maternal feminists did succeed in eroding the strict division between the public and private spheres. However, the arguments that they advanced and the reform activities in which they engaged helped to establish maternal feminism as the dominant discourse within which women's role was to be structured. Despite obtaining the formal legal rights associated with meaningful citizenship, women did not occupy a position of equality in the public sphere. Women entered the public sphere as the embodiment of the private sphere's morality and thus as citizens whose gender differentiated them from the general populace by ascribing to them specific roles and responsibilities.[142] As such, they retained responsibility for the home and all domestic tasks. Consequently, child care was framed as a domestic requirement as opposed to a broad economic and social one and interpreted to mean that children needed a type of care that could only be supplied by a full-time stay-at-home mother.[143] This had a dual effect. First, only those who could hire replacement domestic workers – in other words, white middle class women – could access the public sphere on an equal footing with men, without being forced to work a double day in the public and private spheres. Second, those who did access the public sphere were restricted to traditional "women's" questions; that is, those that were an outgrowth of their maternal function.

Within this gendered notion of citizenship, however, some women were more equal, and hence more powerful, than others. By utilizing their economic and social privilege and their organizational and personal resources to further their vision of an ideal society constructed along lines of class, race, and gender, white middle class women ensured that some women would have more rights than others. Their reform activities, especially those in the area of immigration, were based on a racist conception of who belonged in the Canadian community. Black people, viewed as unassimilable, threatened the homogeneity and unity of the Canadian community. This racism permeated immigration rules and procedures: black women, although not suitable citizens, were suitable servants for white middle class homes. This perception was to guide future immigration policy concerning domestic workers.

With the inception of the Welfare State, the State acceded to many of the reformers' demands for greater State intervention, took over many of their reform activities, including welfare, immigration, and mother's pensions, and built upon them. Ultimately, the State's intervention in areas such as the economy and the private sphere created a new concept of citizenship and citizenship rights derived from policy entitlements. Yet, because these new Welfare State concepts were premised on the ideology of maternal feminism, only some women were able to increase their rights. This occurred at the expense of other, especially black, women.

Notes

1. Carol Bacchi, *Liberation Deferred? The Ideas of the English Canadian Suffragists, 1877-1918* (Canada: University of Toronto Press, 1983), 110.
2. Janine Brodie, *Politics on the Boundaries: Restructuring and the Canadian Women's Movement* (Toronto: Robarts Center for Canadian Studies, 1994), 23. Janine Brodie, *Politics on the Margins: Restructuring and the Canadian Women's Movement* (Nova Scotia: Fernwood Publishing Company, 1995), 29.
3. Janine Brodie, *Politics on the Boundaries: Restructuring and the Canadian Women's Movement* (Toronto: Robarts Center for Canadian Studies, 1994), 23. Janine Brodie, *Politics on the Margins: Restructuring and the Canadian Women's Movement* (Nova Scotia: Fernwood Publishing Company, 1995), 29.
4. Janine Brodie, *Politics on the Margins: Restructuring and the Canadian Women's Movement* (Nova Scotia: Fernwood Publishing Company, 1995), 30.
5. *Ibid.*, 29.
6. *Ibid.*, 34.
7. *Ibid.*
8. Janine Brodie, *Politics on the Boundaries: Restructuring and the Canadian Women's Movement* (Toronto: Robarts Center for Canadian Studies, 1994), 23.
9. *Ibid.*, 26.
10. Iris Marion Young, "Polity and Group Difference: A Critique of the Ideal of Universal Citizenship," *Ethics* 99 (January 1989), 250, 254–5.
11. Janine Brodie, *Politics on the Margins: Restructuring and the Canadian Women's Movement* (Nova Scotia: Fernwood Publishing Company, 1995), 30.
12. This term is taken from Nancy Adamson, Linda Briskin, and Margaret

McPhail, *Feminists Organizing for Change: The Contemporary Women's Movement in Canada* (Toronto: Oxford University Press, 1988), 33. Although this term will be used repeatedly throughout the text, for reasons of simplicity it will not be cited again.

13. Linda Kealey, "Introduction," *A Not Unreasonable Claim: Women and Reform in Canada, 1880s-1920s*, ed. Linda Kealey (Toronto: The Women's Press, 1979), 12. Although this term will be used repeatedly throughout the text, for reasons of simplicity, it will not be cited again.

14. Jane Jenson, cited in Janine Brodie, *Politics on the Margins: Restructuring and the Canadian Women's Movement* (Nova Scotia: Fernwood Publishing Company, 1995), 37.

15. Janine Brodie, *Politics on the Margins: Restructuring and the Canadian Women's Movement* (Nova Scotia: Fernwood Publishing Company, 1995), 37.

16. Jane Errington, "Pioneers and Suffragists," *Changing Patterns: Women in Canada* eds. Sandra Burt, Lorraine Code and Lindsay Dorney (Toronto: McClelland & Stewart, 1990), 57.

17. Jane Errington, "Pioneers and Suffragists," *Changing Patterns: Women in Canada* eds. Sandra Burt, Lorraine Code and Lindsay Dorney (Toronto: McClelland & Stewart, 1990), 57. Starting in the seventeenth century, a married Canadian woman's only legal right was the right to be provided with life's basic necessities. The extent of these depended on the extent of her husband's income. She was not allowed to own property; any property that she owned before marriage was turned over to her husband after the ceremony took place. Furthermore, a married woman had no say in decisions made about her children and she was not allowed to speak in a court of law. Deborah Gorham, "The Canadian Suffragists" *Women in the Canadian Mosaic*, ed. Gwen Matheson (Toronto: Peter Martin Associates Limited, 1976), 28–29.

18. Barb Cameron and Cathy Pike, "Collective Child Care in a Class Society," *Women Unite: An Anthology of the Canadian Women's Movement* (Toronto: Canadian Women's Educational Press, 1972), 87.

19. For example, in the early nineteenth century, it was socially acceptable for an unmarried woman to own and operate a rooming house, pub, or clothing store and for a married woman to carry on her spouse's business upon his death. Jane Errington, "Pioneers and

Suffragists," *Changing Patterns: Women in Canada*, eds. Sandra Burt, Lorraine Code and Lindsay Dorney (Toronto: McClelland & Stewart, 1990), 59. For an in-depth reading of the type of non-traditional labour that women performed and their social status see Janice Potter, "Patriarchy and Paternalism: The Case of Eastern Loyalist Women," *Rethinking Canada: The Promise of Women's History*, eds. Veronica Strong-Boag and Anita Clair Fellman (Canada: Copp Clark Pitman, 1991), 59-72. For a similar profile of Québec women see Jan Noel, "New France: les femmes favoritisées", pages 28-50 in the same volume.

20. Gail G. Campbell, "Disenfranchised but not Quiescent: Women Petitioners in New Brunswick in the Mid-Nineteenth Century," *Rethinking Canada: The Promise of Women's History* eds. Veronica Strong-Boag and Anita Clair Fellman (Toronto: Copp Clark Pitman Ltd, 1991), 81-83, 92.

21. *Ibid.*, 82.

22. Although three quarters of Canada's population lived in rural areas in 1880, by 1921 half of the population lived in urban areas. Carol Bacchi, *Liberation Deferred? The Ideas of the English Canadian Suffragists, 1877-1918* (Canada: University of Toronto Press, 1983), 9.

23. Peggy Morton, "Women's Work is Never Done...Or the Production, Maintenance and Reproduction of Labour Power," *Women Unite: An Anthology of the Canadian Women's Movement* (Toronto: Canadian Women's Educational Press, 1972), 55.

24. Wayne Roberts, "Rocking the Cradle for the World: The New Woman and Maternal Feminism," *A Not Unreasonable Claim: Women and Reform in Canada, 1880s-1920s*, ed. Linda Kealey (Toronto: The Women's Press, 1979), 27.

25. Barb Cameron and Cathy Pike, "Collective Child Care in a Class Society," *Women Unite: An Anthology of the Canadian Women's Movement* (Toronto: Canadian Women's Educational Press, 1972), 87.

26. Jane Errington, "Pioneers and Suffragists," *Changing Patterns: Women in Canada* eds. Sandra Burt, Lorraine Code and Lindsay Dorney (Toronto: McClelland & Stewart, 1990), 58-9.

27. Sylvia Hamilton, "Naming Names, Naming Ourselves: A Survey of Early Black Women in Nova Scotia," *We Are Rooted Here and They Can't Pull Us Up: Essays in African Canadian Women's History*, ed. Peggy Bristow

(Toronto: University of Toronto Press, 1994), 24. For more information about black women's experience in eighteenth and nineteenth century Canada see the following articles in the same volume. Adrienne Shad, "The Lord Seemed to Say Go: Women and the Underground Railroad Movement," pages 39–67. Peggy Bristow, "Whatever You Raise in the Ground You Can Sell it in Chatham: Black Women in Buxton and Chatham," pages 68–95.

28. Dionne Brand, "We Weren't Allowed to Go into Factory Work Until Hitler Started the War: The 1920s to the 1940s," *We Are Rooted Here and They Can't Pull Us Up: Essays in African Canadian Women's History*, ed. Peggy Bristow (Toronto: University of Toronto Press, 1994), 174.

29. Quoted in *ibid.*, 175.

30. In 1870 a woman sustained an injury from a fall on slippery ice. Although the courts would not give her compensation for her broken leg, the verdict granted her husband $500 on the assumption that her labour was worth this amount. The awarding of compensation to the husband rather than the woman typifies the conception that women were no more than chattel, whose labour was the property of men. Sally Mahood, "The Women's Suffrage Movement in Canada and Saskatchewan," *Women Unite: An Anthology of the Canadian Women's Movement* (Toronto: Canadian Women's Educational Press, 1972), 21.

31. Jane Errington, "Pioneers and Suffragists," *Changing Patterns: Women in Canada*, eds. Sandra Burt, Lorraine Code and Lindsay Dorney (Toronto: McClelland & Stewart, 1990), 60.

32. *Ibid.*, 63.

33. Carol Bacchi, *Liberation Deferred? The Ideas of the English Canadian Suffragists, 1877-1918* (Canada: University of Toronto Press, 1983), 16. Productive functions (e.g. dairying, gardening, preserving food, making clothes, quilts, soap and candles) that occupied a large percentage of women's time in an agricultural setting did not exist in urban areas. The fact that these duties were transferred to the public market meant that women had an increase in leisure time. This was compounded by the declining birth rate and a change in the nature of their duties (e.g. running water in urban areas meant that women were no longer required to fetch water in order to wash clothes, dishes, etc.).

34. Linda Kealey, "Introduction," *A Not Unreasonable Claim: Women and Reform in Canada, 1880s-1920s*, ed. Linda Kealey (Toronto: The Women's Press, 1979), 4.

35. Carol Bacchi, *Liberation Deferred? The Ideas of the English Canadian Suffragists, 1877-1918* (Canada: University of Toronto Press, 1983), 10.

36. Although men also engaged in reform activities, the focus in this chapter will be on women's activities for two reasons. First, it was women's involvement in reform activities that led to the rise of maternal feminism. Second, these women were influential in creating the gender, class and race-based social structure in Canada.

37. Barbara Roberts, "'A Work of Empire': Canadian Reformers and British Female Immigration," *A Not Unreasonable Claim: Women and Reform in Canada, 1880s-1920s*, ed. Linda Kealey (Toronto: The Women's Press, 1979), 186-7.

38. Carol Bacchi, *Liberation Deferred? The Ideas of the English Canadian Suffragists, 1877-1918* (Canada: University of Toronto Press, 1983), 105.

39. Mrs. F. H. Torrington, quoted in *ibid.*, 53.

40. *Ibid.*

41. Barbara Roberts, "'A Work of Empire': Canadian Reformers and British Female Immigration," *A Not Unreasonable Claim: Women and Reform in Canada, 1880s-1920s*, ed. Linda Kealey (Toronto: The Women's Press, 1979), 187-8.

42. Rina Cohen, "A Brief History of Racism in Immigration Policies for Recruiting Domestics," *Canadian Women Studies* 14 (1994), 83.

43. Barbara Roberts, "'A Work of Empire': Canadian Reformers and British Female Immigration," *A Not Unreasonable Claim: Women and Reform in Canada, 1880s-1920s*, ed. Linda Kealey (Toronto: The Women's Press, 1979), 185-6.

44. *Ibid.*, 191-2.

45. *Ibid.*, 192

46. *Ibid.*, 194.

47. *Ibid.*, 193, 196.

48. *Ibid.*, 198-9.

49. *Ibid.*, 197.

50. Rina Cohen, "A Brief History of Racism in Immigration Policies for

Recruiting Domestics," *Canadian Women Studies* 14 (1994), 83.

51. Barbara Roberts, "'A Work of Empire': Canadian Reformers and British Female Immigration," *A Not Unreasonable Claim: Women and Reform in Canada, 1880s-1920s*, ed. Linda Kealey (Toronto: The Women's Press, 1979), 198.

52. Grace M. Anderson and William Marr, "Immigration and Social Policy," *Canadian Social Policy*, ed. Shankar A. Yelada (Canada: Wilfred Laurier Press, 1987), 89, 91–2.

53. These consisted of a healthy bank account, good physical condition, guaranteed employment and family already established in Canada. Agnes Calliste, "Race, Gender and Canadian Immigration Policy: Blacks from the Caribbean, 1900–1932," *Journal of Canadian Studies* 28 (Winter 1993–1994), 136.

54. *Ibid.*

55. Vic Satzewich, "Racism and Canadian Immigration Policy: The Government's View of Caribbean Migration, 1962-1966," *Canadian Ethnic Studies* 21 (1989), 79.

56. *Ibid.*

57. *Ibid.*

58. Agnes Calliste, "Race, Gender and Canadian Immigration Policy: Blacks from the Caribbean, 1900–1932," *Journal of Canadian Studies* 28 (Winter 1993–1994), 140.

59. *Ibid.*

60. *Ibid.*, 132.

61. *Ibid.*, 140-1.

62. *Ibid.*, 143.

63. *Ibid.*

64. Canada used Order(s)-in-Council to approve special movements. These were invoked to accept targeted immigration groups who were normally excluded through standard immigration channels but who could help to fill demand for specific types of labour. Patricia Daenzer, *Regulating Class Privilege: Immigrant Domestic Servants in Canada, 1940s-1990s* (Toronto: Canadian Scholars Press, 1993), 41, 44. This mechanism was used repeatedly in subsequent decades to allow certain women to come to Canada as domestic servants.

65. Agnes Calliste, "Race, Gender and Canadian Immigration Policy: Blacks from the Caribbean, 1900–1932," *Journal of Canadian Studies* 28

(Winter 1993–1994), 138, 143.

66. *Ibid.*, 145.

67. Immigration Superintendent, quoted in *ibid.*, 132.

68. Carol Bacchi, *Liberation Deferred? The Ideas of the English Canadian Suffragists, 1877-1918* (Canada: University of Toronto Press, 1983), 10–11, 52.

69. Wayne Roberts, "Rocking the Cradle for the World: The New Woman and Maternal Feminism," *A Not Unreasonable Claim: Women and Reform in Canada, 1880s-1920s,* ed. Linda Kealey (Toronto: The Women's Press, 1979), 18–9.

70. Carol Bacchi, *Liberation Deferred? The Ideas of the English Canadian Suffragists, 1877-1918* (Canada: University of Toronto Press, 1983), 10–11, 87, 92.

71. Wendy Mitchinson, "The WCTU: 'For God Home and Native Land': A Study in Nineteenth-Century Feminism" *A Not Unreasonable Claim: Women and Reform in Canada, 1880s-1920s,* ed. Linda Kealey (Toronto: The Women's Press, 1979), 151. Carol Bacchi, *Liberation Deferred? The Ideas of the English Canadian Suffragists, 1877-1918* (Canada: University of Toronto Press, 1983), 69.

72. Wendy Mitchinson, "The WCTU: 'For God Home and Native Land': A Study in Nineteenth-Century Feminism," *A Not Unreasonable Claim: Women and Reform in Canada, 1880s-1920s,* ed. Linda Kealey (Toronto: The Women's Press, 1979), 154–5. Carol Bacchi, *Liberation Deferred? The Ideas of the English Canadian Suffragists, 1877-1918* (Canada: University of Toronto Press, 1983), 52, 80.

73. Wendy Mitchinson, "The WCTU: 'For God Home and Native Land': A Study in Nineteenth-Century Feminism," *A Not Unreasonable Claim: Women and Reform in Canada, 1880s-1920s,* ed. Linda Kealey (Toronto: The Women's Press, 1979), 155, 163.

74. *Ibid.*, 155–8.

75. Carol Bacchi, *Liberation Deferred? The Ideas of the English Canadian Suffragists, 1877-1918* (Canada: University of Toronto Press, 1983), 72.

76. Wendy Mitchinson, "The WCTU: 'For God Home and Native Land': A Study in Nineteenth-Century Feminism," *A Not Unreasonable Claim: Women and Reform in Canada, 1880s-1920s,* ed. Linda Kealey (Toronto: The Women's Press, 1979), 151.

77. Carol Bacchi, *Liberation Deferred? The Ideas of the English Canadian*

Suffragists, 1877-1918 (Canada: University of Toronto Press, 1983), 70, 74.

78. *Ibid.*, 72.

79. Wendy Mitchinson, "The WCTU: 'For God Home and Native Land': A Study in Nineteenth-Century Feminism," *A Not Unreasonable Claim: Women and Reform in Canada, 1880s-1920s*, ed. Linda Kealey (Toronto: The Women's Press, 1979), 161-2.

80. Carol Bacchi, *Liberation Deferred? The Ideas of the English Canadian Suffragists, 1877-1918* (Canada: University of Toronto Press, 1983), 19, 66.

81. Wendy Mitchinson, "The WCTU: 'For God Home and Native Land': A Study in Nineteenth-Century Feminism," *A Not Unreasonable Claim: Women and Reform in Canada, 1880s-1920s*, ed. Linda Kealey (Toronto: The Women's Press, 1979), 161.

82. Carol Bacchi, *Liberation Deferred? The Ideas of the English Canadian Suffragists, 1877-1918* (Canada: University of Toronto Press, 1983), 94.

83. *Ibid.*, 95.

84. *Ibid.*, 96.

85. *Ibid.*

86. National Council of Women in Canada (1898), "Education for Domesticity," *The Proper Sphere: Woman's Place in Canadian Society*, eds. Ramsey Cook and Wendy Mitchinson (Toronto: Oxford University Press, 1976), 151-3.

87. Carol Bacchi, *Liberation Deferred? The Ideas of the English Canadian Suffragists, 1877-1918* (Canada: University of Toronto Press, 1983), 50.

88. Carol Bacchi, "Divided Allegiances: The Response of Farm and Labour Women to Suffrage," *A Not Unreasonable Claim: Women and Reform in Canada, 1880s-1920s*, ed. Linda Kealey (Toronto: The Women's Press, 1979), 90, 96.

89. Jane Errington, "Pioneers and Suffragists," *Changing Patterns: Women in Canada*, eds. Sandra Burt, Lorraine Code and Lindsay Dorney (Toronto: McClelland & Stewart, 1990), 69. Carol Bacchi, "Divided Allegiances: The Response of Farm and Labour Women to Suffrage," *A Not Unreasonable Claim: Women and Reform in Canada, 1880s-1920s*, ed. Linda Kealey (Toronto: The Women's Press, 1979), 96.

90. Carol Bacchi, *Liberation Deferred? The Ideas of the English Canadian*

Suffragists, 1877-1918 (Canada: University of Toronto Press, 1983), 86-7, 92-3.

91. *Ibid.*, 89, 91.
92. *Ibid.*, 33.
93. *Ibid.*, 57.
94. *Ibid.*
95. *Ibid.*, 26.
96. Frances Brooke wrote and published Canada's first novel in 1769. This novel was written from an unmistakable feminist stance, arguing that women should be given the vote as well as a comprehensive education, and that marriage should be based upon equality between partners. In effect, she argued for gender equality. For further details see Ann Edwards Boutelle, "Frances Brooke's Emily Montague (1769): Canada and Women's Rights," *Rethinking Canada: The Promise of Women's History*, eds. Veronica Strong-Boag and Anita Clair Fellman (Canada: Copp Clark Pitman, 1991), 51-58.
97. Carol Bacchi, *Liberation Deferred? The Ideas of the English Canadian Suffragists, 1877-1918* (Canada: University of Toronto Press, 1983), 26.
98. *Ibid.*, 14-5. Women doctors, such as Stowe, were forced to go to the United States to receive training. In Canada, training facilities which were segregated by sex, with most of the resources allocated to the male facilities, impeded women's ability to practice this profession. Women's entrance into medicine was acceptable only insofar as they remained in subordinate positions; as such, professional nursing, based on a notion of self-sacrifice, developed as an acceptable profession for women in the nineteenth century. Similarly, although women were accepted in journalism, they tended to be segregated, working mostly on the women's pages. Wayne Roberts, "Rocking the Cradle for the World: The New Woman and Maternal Feminism," *A Not Unreasonable Claim: Women and Reform in Canada, 1880s-1920s*, ed. Linda Kealey (Toronto: The Women's Press, 1979), 31-7.
99. Carol Bacchi, *Liberation Deferred? The Ideas of the English Canadian Suffragists, 1877-1918* (Canada: University of Toronto Press, 1983), 27, 29.
100. Carol Bacchi, *Liberation Deferred? The Ideas of the English Canadian Suffragists, 1877-1918* (Canada: University of Toronto Press, 1983), 31. The steady commodification of domestic production meant that

more women were required to work outside the home in order to earn a living wage; women of a better class tended to opt for white collar employment, which provided better remuneration and had defined hours of work, and not domestic work as the former. Yet they were still treated as a "readily exploitable resource"; their limited skills, prolific numbers and limited number of available options ensured that they remained in a vulnerable and exploitable position. Veronica Strong–Boag, "Ever a Crusader: Nellie McClung, First-Wave Feminist," *Rethinking Canada: The Promise of Women's History*, eds. Veronica Strong–Boag and Anita Clair Fellman (Canada: Copp Clark Pitman, 1991), 310.

101. Carol Bacchi, *Liberation Deferred? The Ideas of the English Canadian Suffragists, 1877-1918* (Canada: University of Toronto Press, 1983), 120. There was one attempt to form a working class woman's suffrage association in 1912, but it was brief and unsuccessful. Wayne Roberts, "Rocking the Cradle for the World: The New Woman and Maternal Feminism," *A Not Unreasonable Claim: Women and Reform in Canada, 1880s-1920s*, ed. Linda Kealey (Toronto: The Women's Press, 1979), 41

102. *Ibid.*, 90–1.

103. *Ibid.*, 30–1. It is interesting to note that the truly upper class initiated an anti-suffrage campaign and, led by Mrs. H. D. Warren, established a women's Anti-Enfranchisement League. These women were wary of the democratic system and perceived it as a structure that undermined Canada's ability to create an organic society based on the family. The League felt that granting women the vote would undermine the family as the basic unit of society by dividing it in two. Moreover, they believed that women's political participation would detract from their role as mother, furthering the ills that plagued the race: a declining birth rate and an increasing divorce rate. They believed that the family required only one vote; that of the male head of the household. Wayne Roberts, "Rocking the Cradle for the World: The New Woman and Maternal Feminism," *A Not Unreasonable Claim: Women and Reform in Canada, 1880s-1920s*, ed. Linda Kealey (Toronto: The Women's Press, 1979), 26. Carol Bacchi, *Liberation Deferred? The Ideas of the English Canadian Suffragists, 1877-1918* (Canada: University of Toronto Press, 1983), 47–49.

104. The National Council of Women in Canada, quoted in Deborah Gorham, "The Canadian Suffragists," *Women in the Canadian Mosaic*, ed. Gwen Matheson (Toronto: Peter Martin Associates Limited, 1976), 24–5.

105. Wayne Roberts, "Rocking the Cradle for the World: The New Woman and Maternal Feminism," *A Not Unreasonable Claim: Women and Reform in Canada, 1880s-1920s* ed. Linda Kealey (Toronto: The Women's Press, 1979), 21–2.

106. For a glimpse of Stowe–Gullen's views see her 1904 article, "A Woman is a Citizen," *The Proper Sphere: Woman's Place in Canadian Society*, ed. Wendy Mitchinson and Ramsey Cook (Toronto: Oxford University Press, 1976), 258–65.

107. Deborah Gorham, "Flora MacDonald Denison: Canadian Feminist," *A Not Unreasonable Claim: Women and Reform in Canada, 1880s-1920s*, ed. Linda Kealey (Toronto: The Women's Press, 1979), 47, 49, 62. Carol Bacchi, *Liberation Deferred? The Ideas of the English Canadian Suffragists, 1877-1918* (Canada: University of Toronto Press, 1983), 30–1.

108. Carol Bacchi, *Liberation Deferred? The Ideas of the English Canadian Suffragists, 1877-1918* (Canada: University of Toronto Press, 1983), 31, 35.

109. Although the National Council of Women in Canada endorsed suffrage, the decision was far from unanimous: the resolution was passed by a vote of 71 to 51. Carol Bacchi, *Liberation Deferred? The Ideas of the English Canadian Suffragists, 1877-1918* (Canada: University of Toronto Press, 1983), 17.

110. Carol Bacchi, *Liberation Deferred? The Ideas of the English Canadian Suffragists, 1877-1918* (Canada: University of Toronto Press, 1983), 31–2.

111. Nellie McClung, quoted in Sylvia Bashevkin, "Independence Versus Partisanship: Dilemmas in the Political History of Women in English Canada," *Rethinking Canada: The Promise of Women's History*, eds. Veronica Strong–Boag and Anita Clair Fellman (Canada: Copp Clark Pitman, 1991), 421–2.

112. Wayne Roberts, "Rocking the Cradle for the World: The New Woman and Maternal Feminism," *A Not Unreasonable Claim: Women and Reform in Canada, 1880s-1920s*, ed. Linda Kealey (Toronto: The Women's Press, 1979), 23–4. Deborah Gorham, "The Canadian Suffragists," *Women in the Canadian Mosaic* ed. Gwen Matheson (Toronto: Peter Martin

Associates Limited, 1976), 26.

113. Wayne Roberts, "Rocking the Cradle for the World: The New Woman and Maternal Feminism," *A Not Unreasonable Claim: Women and Reform in Canada, 1880s-1920s* ed. Linda Kealey (Toronto: The Women's Press, 1979), 24.

114. Carol Bacchi, *Liberation Deferred? The Ideas of the English Canadian Suffragists, 1877-1918* (Canada: University of Toronto Press, 1983), 38.

115. Wayne Roberts, "Rocking the Cradle for the World: The New Woman and Maternal Feminism," *A Not Unreasonable Claim: Women and Reform in Canada, 1880s-1920s,* ed. Linda Kealey (Toronto: The Women's Press, 1979), 24.

116. Carol Bacchi, *Liberation Deferred? The Ideas of the English Canadian Suffragists, 1877-1918* (Canada: University of Toronto Press, 1983), 11, 48.

117. "In 1916 she asked Borden to give only British-born women [the right] to vote to offset the lower moral tone of the electorate caused by 'the going away of so many of our best and most public spirited men'". Carol Bacchi, *Liberation Deferred? The Ideas of the English Canadian Suffragists, 1877-1918* (Canada: University of Toronto Press, 1983), 140.

118. *Ibid.,* 53-4.

119. Mrs. Gordon Grant (1888), "The Vote to do Away with Drink," *The Proper Sphere: Women's Place in Canadian Society,* eds. Ramsey Cook and Wendy Mitchinson (Toronto: Oxford University Press, 1976), 257.

120. Carol Bacchi, *Liberation Deferred? The Ideas of the English Canadian Suffragists, 1877-1918* (Canada: University of Toronto Press, 1983), 50, 54.

121. Carol Bacchi, "Divided Allegiances: The Response of Farm and Labour Women to Suffrage," *A Not Unreasonable Claim: Women and Reform in Canada, 1880s-1920s* (Toronto: The Women's Press, 1979), 90.

122. Veronica Strong-Boag, "Ever a Crusader: Nellie McClung, First-Wave Feminist," *Rethinking Canada: The Promise of Women's History,* eds. Veronica Strong-Boag and Anita Clair Fellman (Canada: Copp Clark Pitman, 1991), 314.

123. For examples of both these types of arguments see Ramsey Cook and Wendy Mitchinson eds. *The Proper Sphere: Women's Place in Canadian Society* (Toronto: Oxford University Press, 1976).

124. Carol Bacchi, *Liberation Deferred? The Ideas of the English Canadian*

Suffragists, 1877-1918 (Canada: University of Toronto Press, 1983), 120.

125. Carol Bacchi, "Divided Allegiances: The Response of Farm and Labour Women to Suffrage," *A Not Unreasonable Claim: Women and Reform in Canada, 1880s-1920s*, ed. Linda Kealey (Toronto: The Women's Press, 1979), 96-8.

126. Deborah Gorham, "The Canadian Suffragists," *Women in the Canadian Mosaic*, ed. Gwen Matheson (Toronto: Peter Martin Associates Limited, 1976), 39.

127. Carol Bacchi, *Liberation Deferred? The Ideas of the English Canadian Suffragists, 1877-1918* (Canada: University of Toronto Press, 1983), 127-9. For more information about working class and farm women's role in the suffrage movement see: Carol Bacchi, "Divided Allegiances: The Response of Farm and Labour Women to Suffrage," *A Not Unreasonable Claim: Women and Reform in Canada, 1880s-1920s*, ed. Linda Kealey (Toronto: The Women's Press, 1979), 89-107; chapter eight in Carol Bacchi, *Liberation Deferred? The Ideas of the English Canadian Suffragists, 1877-1918* (Canada: University of Toronto Press, 1983); Sally Mahood, "The Women's Suffrage Movement in Canada and Saskatchewan," *Women Unite: An Anthology of the Canadian Women's Movement* (Toronto: Canadian Women's Educational Press, 1972), 21-30; and Janice Newton, *The Feminist Challenge to the Canadian Left, 1900-1918* (Canada: McGill-Queen's University Press, 1995).

128. Carol Bacchi, *Liberation Deferred? The Ideas of the English Canadian Suffragists, 1877-1918* (Canada: University of Toronto Press, 1983), 38.

129. The perception that women's involvement in the war effort was temporary justified women's lesser remuneration: they were paid 20-30% less than men. Jane Errington, "Pioneers and Suffragists," *Changing Patterns: Women in Canada*, eds. Sandra Burt, Lorraine Code and Lindsay Dorney (Toronto: McClelland & Stewart, 1990), 73.

130. Carol Bacchi, *Liberation Deferred? The Ideas of the English Canadian Suffragists, 1877-1918* (Canada: University of Toronto Press, 1983), 142.

131. *Ibid.*, 137-41. Matheson and V. E. Lang, "Nellie McClung: Not a Nice Woman," *Women in the Canadian Mosaic*, ed. Gwen Matheson (Toronto: Peter Martin Associates Limited, 1976), 13.

132. Sylvia Bashevkin, "Independence Versus Partisanship: Dilemmas in the Political History of Women in English Canada," *Rethinking Canada: The Promise of Women's History*, eds. Veronica Strong-Boag and Anita

Clair Fellman (Canada: Copp Clark Pitman, 1991), 422.

133.*Ibid.*, 425. The Woman's Party's platform listed: "equal pay for equal work, equal marriage laws including equal conditions of divorce, equality of parental rights, raising the age of consent and equal homesteading privileges" – reforms that would benefit all women. Carol Bacchi, *Liberation Deferred? The Ideas of the English Canadian Suffragists, 1877-1918* (Canada: University of Toronto Press, 1983), 131. Despite this platform, many women criticized the party on other grounds, viewing the party as representing women of the urban middle class. Its platform of "war till victory, stronger imperial ties and opposition to labour unionization" made it unpopular with farm women and working class women. Both of these groups of women saw the men of their class as their allies. Carol Bacchi, "Divided Allegiances: The Response of Farm and Labour Women to Suffrage," *A Not Unreasonable Claim: Women and Reform in Canada, 1880s-1920s*, ed. Linda Kealey (Toronto: The Women's Press, 1979), 105.

134.The Federated Women's Institutes of Canada and the National Council of Women in Canada, both middle class organizations, were included in these groups.

135.Sylvia Bashevkin, "Independence Versus Partisanship: Dilemmas in the Political History of Women in English Canada," *Rethinking Canada: The Promise of Women's History*, eds. Veronica Strong–Boag and Anita Clair Fellman (Canada: Copp Clark Pitman, 1991), 428.

136.Quoted in *Ibid.*, 429.

137. *Ibid.* , 429.

138.*Ibid.*, 424.

139. Jane Errington, "Pioneers and Suffragists," *Changing Patterns: Women in Canada*, eds. Sandra Burt, Lorraine Code and Lindsay Dorney (Toronto: McClelland & Stewart, 1990), 74.

140. Carol Bacchi, *Liberation Deferred? The Ideas of the English Canadian Suffragists, 1877-1918* (Canada: University of Toronto Press, 1983), 145.

141. Sylvia Bashevkin, "Independence Versus Partisanship: Dilemmas in the Political History of Women in English Canada," *Rethinking Canada: The Promise of Women's History*, eds. Veronica Strong–Boag and Anita Clair Fellman (Canada: Copp Clark Pitman, 1991), 424, 426. Carol Bacchi, *Liberation Deferred? The Ideas of the English Canadian Suffragists,*

1877-1918 (Canada: University of Toronto Press, 1983), 147.

142. Janine Brodie, *Politics on the Margins: Restructuring and the Canadian Women's Movement* (Nova Scotia: Fernwood Publishing Company, 1995), 37.

143. Nancy Fraser, "Talking About Needs: Interpretive Contests as Political Conflicts in Welfare–State Societies," *Ethics* 99 (January 1989), 300.

Chapter 2

UNEQUAL DEVELOPMENT
Black Women Enter the Homes that White Women Leave for the Market

Between 1929 and 1967, Canadian women occupied a position of toleration. According to Trimble (1990), women's status had improved under the law once they were granted citizenship and citizenship rights in 1929. The line between the public and the private was beginning to shift as women were starting to be seen in the public sphere. However, the legal admission of women as participants in the public sphere was precisely that – a legality. In practice, the public–private divide remained entrenched with all its trappings of sex–role stereotypes and their associated responsibilities. Only those women who were able to hire replacement home workers were able to access the public sphere on an equal footing with men. These were largely white middle class women. Women of colour and working class women who entered the competitive marketplace remained responsible for all domestic tasks and thus were forced to work a double day.

During this period, Canada underwent a period of "restructuring" in which it changed from a Laissez–Faire to a Welfare State.[1] According to Jones (1990), citizenship and citizenship rights came to be determined by the number of social policy entitlements an individual could lay claim to. These discrepancies between individuals in turn created a citizenry divided by class[2] and race. Immigration policy regarding domestic workers contin-ued to restrict black women's access to citizenship and policy entitlements throughout this period.

As Trimble (1990) has explained, in keeping with the tenets of liberal pluralism which require the participation of the periphery in the politics of the center, women were granted full citizenship rights in 1929. This milestone was reached partly due to the pre-vailing idea of the individual having certain rights. Rights that were exclusively enjoyed by men were now granted to women who had been legally declared individuals. However, while legal barriers were removed, the State made no effort toward actively encouraging women to participate in politics or the economy. Women participants in the public sphere were faced with a great deal of resistance. At best, they were tolerated for their aberrant behavior.

Trimble (1990) also documents that despite these intangible barriers, any discrepancy in women's and men's participation in politics was seen as evidence confirming the belief that women's natural place was in the home. Those women who did participate in the nation's political life could not be separated from the private sphere and hence were allowed to deal only with issues traditionally perceived as belonging to women's preserve. This perception allowed for a continuation of policies that restricted women's access to resources necessary to participate fully in public life. This situation lasted until 1967 when the Royal Commission on the Status of Women was established. At that point, it was acknowledged that not only did women have a right to participate in the public sphere but the State was obliged to facilitate this participation.

During this period, the Keynesian Welfare State emerged, born of society's belief that the government should ensure that citizens' basic needs were met and that economic activity be reg-ulated by broad-based policies that would benefit the maximum number of citizens. Within this particular State form, citizenship status allowed all Canadians to make legitimate claims on the social safety net.[3] Yet Keynesian Welfare State social measures were premised on, and aimed to further, the existing public-private divide and traditional familial structure of "...a stable working and middle class, a nuclear family supported by a male breadwinner, a family wage, a dependent wife and children, and women's unpaid domestic labour."[4] The State's support of this particular family form fit into the maternal feminist framework that dictated that women were mothers first and foremost, whose proper place was in the home.

Welfare policy did not treat women as a distinct group that possessed specific social and economic concerns. Rather, the State considered them only within the context of motherhood. When developing social policy, the State assumed that there was no distinction between women's economic and social interests and those of their families, and enacted policies in order to uphold the status quo: a stay-at-home mother supported by a working father and an economic system premised on women's domestic donation. The State ensured the survival of this familial structure by means of legislating workers' rights, such as collective bargaining, and by implementing social entitlements associated with the Keynesian Welfare State.[5] These social measures were designed to allow the State to fill the void should the desired family structure fail to emerge or to function properly. Within this context, child care was treated as a specific domestic requirement, rather than a broad economic and social one. Children, it was understood, required care that could only be provided by full-time stay-at-home mothers and the solution was framed in individualist terms, taking the form of Mother's Pensions and child tax credits.[6] For those women who could afford it, in other words, white middle and upper class women, the individualist solution took the form of hiring domestic workers.

Hiring domestics was possible due to State policies that were enacted with respect to domestic workers. Until the war years, British and black Canadian women continued to work in domestic service. In the post-war period, both these groups of women began to turn to other areas of employment in the public sector, where conditions of work and rates of pay were more attractive. As a result, there was a scarcity of domestic servants in Canada and the State began to turn towards non-traditional (non-British) source countries for a new supply of labour. Black women, however, were desired neither as citizens nor as mothers. Although the State, in 1955, allowed black women from the Caribbean to enter Canada as domestics, they were not granted full citizenship rights. These domestics, unlike their British counterparts, were forced to work for low pay under increasingly restrictive conditions without labour, political, or civil protection and liberties. Regressive policies were implemented at roughly the same time that Canadian women began to mobilize for more rights.

Although the entitlements Canadian women could legitimately claim were defined by the State as ones that would allow them to effectively carry out their roles as mothers, they were able to mobilize and make certain political demands, such as extending existing social services. Women's organizations, often State-funded, began to multiply, ultimately providing women with a vehicle to pressure the State for greater intervention geared towards improving women's own economic and social conditions, even as they emphasized the needs of their families and their own maternal role.[7]

These women's organizations, however, were constructed along lines of race and class. White middle class women's organizations were at the forefront of the movement that pressed the State for change. These women believed that the Keynesian Welfare State was a benevolent body that could and would address the structural problems that had hindered women's ability to attain economic and social parity with their male counterparts.[8] These women demanded State action to effect change without stating the parameters within which change should occur. Consequently, the State advanced solutions framed within prevailing assumptions about familial structures, the gender order, and race. By accepting these terms, middle class white women effectively truncated the possibility of any real change in the gender order and in gender relations. Women would continue to be responsible for domestic work and women of colour would continue to be imported to perform it under increasingly restrictive conditions. This chapter will trace the process which culminated in this position.

I. The Terrible Thirties: The Great Depression and a Reinforcement of the Traditional Gender Order

As the prosperous 1920s gave way to the terrible 1930s, women found themselves under increasing pressure to embrace their new "profession" of motherhood and homemaker. Well-entrenched assumptions about appropriate gender roles meant that the few available jobs went to men, thereby allowing them to fulfill their traditional function as the family's supporter.[9] Canada's immigration regulations became increasingly restrictive once the Great Depression began in 1930–31, with only eighty-nine Caribbean domestics allowed to enter the country. During the next decade, immigration was virtually suspended.[10] The few domestic workers who immigrated were from Europe and were hired as contract workers.[11]

The demand for domestic workers decreased. Most available domestic jobs were filled by white women who wanted to supplement their family's meager earnings – single mothers and married women whose husbands were unable to find work tended to seek out domestic work.[12] Black women in cities such as Montreal and Toronto continued to have restricted job opportunities. Yet, as Brand (1994) argues, of those who could find work, at least eighty percent were employed in domestic service. These women were liable to such arbitrary demands as waiving their right to time off, being forced to work sixteen hour days, and being paid in material goods instead of wages. The racism that constricted their job opportunities ensured that black women could be easily exploited. Black women's limited employment opportunities lasted until the end of World War Two.[13]

II. World War Two: Breaking Traditional Gender Barriers as an Emergency Measure

Between 1939 and 1945, women were recruited to work in the war industries. The national government fostered their participation. In 1942, the National Selective Service registration recognized the potential of Canadian women as a great untapped labour reserve.[14] Soon after, targeted groups of women were pulled into the "armed forces, defense industries, service sector and agriculture".[15] The home front industrial war efforts enlisted the help of first young single women, followed by married women without children and then mothers.[16] These women were primarily white. Although some black women entered the public sphere via clerical and factory labour, racism continued to permeate the public sphere. Many black women continued to work as domestics well into the war.[17] During the war, domestic servants were in short supply and it is not unlikely that black Canadian women helped to fill the demand.

Canadian society did not see women's participation in the paid workforce as a permanent development. As in World War One, the public sphere embraced women only insofar as wartime scarcity dictated. Although some women received training for particular occupations in government–sponsored programs, the goal of this training was to help the nation attain its wartime objectives, not to improve women's participation in the work-force. Because many more women were gainfully employed, the government was forced to establish child care centers and give married women tax concessions.[18] These measures were designed to help women carry out their traditional maternal functions in the context of a national emergency. At no point were they seen as permanent measures.[19] Once the war ended and women's work in the public sphere was no longer valuable to the nation, these State-sponsored child care facilities were shut down and federal statutes were re-organized according to pre-war regulations.[20]

During the war, immigration was restricted to Great Britain. The federal government justified these restrictive immigration regulations by pointing to the many Canadian men and women who would be shunted out of war-related industry and be in need of new employment come the end of the war – it was important to save the jobs for them.[21] From 1942 until 1945, Canadian women, attempting to acquire black domestic workers, requested that the Department of Citizenship and Immigration import black Caribbean women. Although these women were widely available and inexpensive to employ, the Department of Citizenship and Immigration refused the requests. This position was based on the belief that Canadian women, once pushed out of the paid work force, would return to their homes and resume their domestic duties.[22] As the director stated in a memorandum:

> After the war there will be thousands of Canadian
> girls who have been working in war industries of
> one sort or another who will have to be absorbed
> in the economic life of the country and if there is
> a strong demand for houseworkers, it will provide
> an important means for their absorption...[23]

Between 1945 and May 1946, the government and industry wanted to encourage married women to resume their traditional private roles. As a result, 90 000 Canadian women found themselves newly unemployed.[24] Sexual stereotypes prevailed. Although women had played an integral economic role during war-time their social status was not altered.[25] Women continued to be responsible for domestic work. Those who wanted to enter the public sphere were required to find replacement home workers or work a double day.

At the same time, however, given the economic and industrial expansion of the post-war era, the Canadian government realized that a larger work force would be necessary. Women began to be viewed as a reserve labour force that could be called upon, when

needed, to leave their traditional private–sphere duties[26], including those Canadian women (both black and white) who had
traditionally performed domestic work in private homes.
Consequently, the Department of Citizenship and Immigration's
belief that the shortage of domestic workers was temporary
proved to be mistaken. Even after women were removed from
the formal marketplace, the demand for domestics did not
decrease. New employment opportunities created a scarcity of
domestic servants. In 1945 and 1946 the demand for domestic
workers in both urban and rural areas could not be filled.[27]

In addition, British women who had traditionally immigrated
and worked within this category were no longer willing to do so.
The increase in occupational categories open to them in their
home country meant that service in private homes was no longer
desirable. British women who did immigrate as domestic workers
tended to move quickly into the newly available areas of
employment that provided better remuneration and established
hours of work.[28] These developments, combined with international pressures placed on Canada to accept displaced
Europeans, resulted in a marked shift in immigration policy.

III. 1947, The Year of a New Immigration Policy: Non-British Immigrants Designated for the Occupation of Domestic Work

After the war, Canadian society demonstrated a marked increase
in its level of xenophobia.[29] As a result, Canadian immigration
quotas were fixed at existing levels.[30] However, two groups were
pressuring Canada to expand its immigration policy. Affluent
Canadians still wanted immigration procedures to be relaxed to
permit the recruitment of a new source of domestic labour and
the international community was pressing the Canadian State to
do its part in European post–war reconstruction by allowing

displaced Europeans to immigrate.[31] In order to bring new immigrants into Canada without causing social problems, the State had to assure Canadians that the new groups would not usurp their place in the labour force. As a result, although Canada agreed to accept some of the displaced Europeans in 1947, it was within specific parameters – as domestic workers. This solution satisfied all groups involved. The supply of domestic workers would increase and refugees would occupy an occupational category that was unattractive to Canadians.[32]

The Canadian Cabinet authorized for entry the first group of 3 000 domestic workers in June of 1947.[33] These domestics, like the Caribbean domestics of 1910–11, entered Canada through special Order-in-Council group movements and not through regular immigration procedures. And, unlike other immigrants working in the public sphere who dealt directly with their employers in contractual matters, these workers were required to deal with the Department of Labour. This body forced the incoming immigrants to sign a pledge stating that they would remain in service for a minimum of one year. This term of bondage was part of an employment contract that guaranteed domestics no rights except the right to apply for Canadian citizenship as soon as they set foot on Canadian soil. This agreement did not provide domestic workers with designated holidays nor did it protect them from abuse. The employers, moreover, were not required to sign a similar contract outlining their rights and obligations.[34]

As a result, domestic workers were dependent on employers who were chosen by the Minister of Labour. Size of weekly pay and hours of work were supposed to be determined according to the norms of the employer's residential region. Yet the actual terms of employment were to be worked out between the domestic and her employer. This often meant that domestics worked more than forty hours per week, as no limit was definitively set by the Minister of Labour. Despite this type of frequent abuse, domestics were not allowed to switch jobs without the Department's approval. This lack of protection was compounded by denying them social safety net measures accorded to all workers employed in Canada's public sphere. On average, foreign domestic workers earned thirty-five dollars a month. Yet, unlike other men and women in the Canadian workforce, they had neither job mobility nor access to Unemployment Insurance and Family Allowances.[35] This was possible as a result of two factors: immigrants' need to access Canadian citizenship and entrenched values about the worth of domestic labour.

In 1949, Cabinet allowed formerly excluded nationality groups (Western and Southern Europeans) to immigrate to Canada by Order-in-Council. Such measures applied on a one-time basis to an entire group. Yet these individuals were required to work in service for one year. While both men and women were included in this program, different standards and guidelines prevailed. Men were expected to send for their families shortly after they came to Canada, while the State desired young, single women without any familial obligations.[36] Consequently, single mothers were rejected from this domestic worker program. Men were paid more than women, in keeping with a division of labour ordered according to established sex-role stereotypes. While men tended to work outside the home as gardeners, drivers and yardmen, women continued to be relegated to jobs in which they were required to perform tasks traditionally associated with women's roles and responsibilities – childcare, cooking, and house-keeping.[37]

The new European immigrants signed the Minister of Labour's contract. Yet, once they obtained landed status, most left domestic service as soon as the chance to work in other employment areas arose. Since landed status gave them the right to change occupations, these domestics were not bonded to their employers. Canada's perpetual problem of a lack of domestic workers pushed the State to utilize the family reunification clause of the Immigration Act to this end. In accordance with this clause, Canada agreed to pay for the wives of newly immigrated refugees to come to Canada, provided the women worked as domestic servants.[38]

By 1951, there were 73 900 domestics employed in Canada, 71 700 of whom were women.[39] Although Canada had relaxed its immigration criteria regarding non-British European domestic workers, there continued to be a shortage of domestic servants. By the early 1950s, Canada's offers of immigrant status in exchange for time served in domestic service paled in comparison to the employment opportunities created in Europe's post-war economic recovery.[40]

At the same time, the number of Canadian women, including wives and mothers, entering the paid workforce was increasing. In 1951, women composed 24.5% of the work force[41] and married women composed 9.6% of the work force.[42] Married women were not able to access the economy on an equal footing with their male counterparts since they remained responsible for domestic work. Not only were their salaries lower than men's but if they had paid for child care services, they were unable to deduct the expense from their taxes. Income tax often cancelled out the small profit these women had accrued.[43]

Consequently, the demand for domestic workers willing to work for wages lower than those given to regular child care increased. Although Canada instituted Assisted Passage loans in 1953 to attract Europeans[44], few Europeans were willing to immigrate as domestics workers. This resulted in a programmatic shift in immigration policy. Black women from the Caribbean would be accepted as domestic workers but under increasingly restrictive conditions. Once again, paid low wages and forced to serve in domestic work for a specific length of time, they were to provide a bonded work force that would enable some Canadian women to join the paid labour force on a more equitable footing with their male counterparts.

IV. The Second West Indies Domestic Scheme: 1955-68

Despite having acknowledged the severe labour shortage, especially in domestic work, the Canadian government repeat-edly rejected requests made by private Canadian citizens (includ-ing future Prime Minister Pearson) for domestic workers and farm labourers from the British West Indies.[45] Because black immi-grants were seen as unassimilable and unable to adapt to life in Canada, up until 1955 Canadian immigration regulations restricted the number of blacks allowed to enter with permanent resident status – one hundred per year was the sum total for all classes.[46] In June 1955, Cabinet allowed one hundred black Caribbean women to enter Canada as domestic workers.[47] This policy shift was the result of several factors and was differentiated from previous quotas in several ways.

First, the international community was urging Canada to shift its position in international relations towards more contact with the third world and away from its existing Eurocentric stance. Second, the black immigrant community in Canada was pressing the State to allow more black women in and to phase out discriminatory regulations. Third, as in the Scheme of 1910-11, private Canadian employers vacationing in the Caribbean were placing demands on the State to accept Caribbean women to work in domestic service, citing them as an inexpensive and abundant source of labour. Last, Caribbean governments were pressuring Canada to allow some of their citizens to enter Canada to work.[48] It was this last group that tilted the balance in favour of changing immigration regulations.

Canada had several investments in the Caribbean in the form of banks, aluminum, and bauxite, all of which were important the Canadian economy.[49] Canada's discriminatory immigration regulations were placing a strain on its relationships with the various British West Indies governments and, consequently, threatening its economic interests. Thus, in February of 1955, when Caribbean governments proposed accepting their citizens through a regulated domestic scheme, Canada acquiesced.[50]

In addition to the aim of preserving trade relations, the State effected this policy change for several other practical reasons. First, it was believed that Caribbean women would remain in domestic service for a longer period of time than white women. As Canadian immigration officials argued, "...[T]here is little danger of these girls, once admitted, leaving domestic employment to seek higher wages in industry for there are very limited opportunities for them in Canada other than domestic service."[51] Second, it would not cost the Canadian government more than it had already spent, since administrative structures designed to handle the women's reception and distribution were already in place. Third, Caribbean governments agreed to create and pay for domestic science training programs in order to ensure high quality workers. Finally, Caribbean governments offered to take on the administrative task of processing the immigrants and pay for the cost of returning any domestic worker found to be unsuitable to her home country, thereby decreasing Canadian costs.[52]

Women admitted to this program were subject to several requirements. They had to be young (aged twenty-one to thirty-five), unmarried, healthy, possess at least five years of institutional education, and promise to remain in service for a minimum of one year. They were excluded from Unemployment Insurance and, unlike domestic workers from preferred countries such as Britain, they were not eligible for assisted passage loans, although persons admitted would be granted landed status.[53]

The Canadian government clearly stated that the scheme would be terminated if any of the Caribbean women failed to finish their allotted year in service.[54] In the early years of the scheme, Caribbean governments, reluctant to assume deportation costs, sent their best citizens to Canada. The women chosen to take part in the scheme thus tended to have a professional background. Caribbean female professionals were admitted to Canada as unskilled labourers.[55] The Caribbean governments' careful selection of women to take part in this scheme meant that they actively helped to shape a policy that operated to their disadvantage. Their most valued asset – educated citizens – was sent to Canada to maintain its labour force.

The scheme's terms were thus inequitably biased in favour of the Canadian State and employers. Canada was not burdened with a group of unskilled women who would become a social liability. Since any woman who did not complete her term of employment or became ill prior to attaining citizenship was to be deported at the expense of Caribbean governments, these women would not be a burden on Canadian citizens. Moreover, although Caribbean women were granted the right of landed status, unlike European domestics who entered under less restrictive conditions and possessed mobility rights, their forced term of service meant that Canadian employers were guaranteed a source of domestic labour. This inequity was possible due to the Caribbean nations' depressed economic conditions and high unemployment rates. They needed Canada as a safety valve for those citizens who were unemployed and they relied on domestic workers' remittances to decrease the Caribbean nations' fiscal burden.[56]

The program had become increasingly popular with both Canadian and Caribbean governments and expanded in scope. In contrast to 1955, when only one hundred female domestics and two islands were involved, 1959 was notable for the involvement of eleven territories and two hundred and eighty female domestics.[57] Because women in this program were pre-placed in employment and Canadian employers could request specific women, Caribbean women in the islands who lacked marketable skills were placing ads in Canadian newspapers. In essence, these women were competing to enter Canada under restrictive requirements in order to gain citizenship status and a more lucrative employment. By 1960, however, Canadian officials were expressing the view that the established requirements of training and assured service for a period of one year were not sufficient. Domestic workers who completed their year of service moved out of private domestic work as quickly as possible.[58]

Moreover, the State voiced concerns about the fact that once Caribbean women attained citizenship they tended to sponsor dependents and relatives who lacked skills, thereby placing a social burden on Canada.[59] As the Deputy Minister stated in 1964

> ...Promiscuity is widespread here [Caribbean] and it is quite usual especially in the lower echelons of the social scale,...I should emphasize perhaps more than I have...that the most undesirable feature of a flow of unsponsored immigrants who are relatively unskilled is their capacity to generate a sponsored flow of a startling high volume... immigrants of dubious economic value to Canada and who may well cause insoluble social problems.[60]

In 1962 and 1967, immigration laws were changed to ostensibly universal and neutral selection criteria. At the same time, however, they served to place greater restrictions on Caribbean women[61], thereby serving to assuage the fears expressed by officials.

Canada intended to evaluate potential immigrants on the basis of their expertise or labour experience in relation to Canadian labour requirements. To this end, it designed a point system that would obviate group movements.[62] However, immigration continued to be structured around racist stereotypes[63], and Caribbean women continued to enter through the domestic scheme under increasingly restrictive conditions. In 1961, the educational requirement for Caribbean domestics was elevated from grade eight to high school in order to avert the influx of Caribbeans who possessed few marketable skills.[64] Quotas for Caribbean domestics increased from 250 to 500 in 1966 to deflect demands for equal treatment of Caribbean citizens. Women from the Caribbean region continued to enter Canada through group movements until 1968.[65]

Education, training, skills and other credentials were listed in the new Immigration Act of 1967 as prerequisites for access to Canada. Officials could no longer justifiable cite race as a reason for barring individuals entry. A point system was introduced and domestic workers were to be evaluated based on the number of points they accrued. Despite the ostensible neutrality of selection procedures, Caribbean women were subjected to different procedures than were white women.[66] As Daenzer (1993) documents, the new system was structured so that Canadian occupations were assessed according to the market's level of demand. A higher level of demand translated into more points and more immigration to fill those occupations whenever Canadians were unable, or unwilling, to undertake these jobs. The demand rating for all categories of domestic work, except nannies and nurse-maids, was lowered in 1968 without providing evidence that demand had, in fact, decreased.[67] Although historically domestic work had a high demand level and thus a high immigration level, the implementation of a two-tiered rating scale meant that Caribbean women were placed at a disadvantage.

The Caribbean region, unlike Britain, did not have formal institutions to train nannies and nursemaids. As a result, Caribbean women, who were unlikely to accumulate points on factors such as financial resources, education, skills training, and "personal suitability"[68] – a term that granted officials discretionary power over potential immigrants – were largely unable to amass the required points to enter Canada in a skilled domestic profession and thus obtain citizenship.[69] Instead, they continued to enter as domestic workers who were subject to different selection procedures than were white women, including the requirements that they be unattached romantically, without dependents, young, experienced or formally educated in domestic "science", and had expressed a desire to work in service.[70]

Most of the Caribbean women who entered Canada and attained citizenship status left private domestic service as soon as possible.[71] Those with skills entered occupations that provided better remuneration. Others, lacking marketable skills, moved into the public sector where they performed similar labour but under better conditions. Primarily, the public sector gave them access to the protective regulations instituted by the Keynesian Welfare State. Domestic workers employed in private homes did not have a right to a minimum wage and were excluded from annual vacation legislation (except in Saskatchewan and Prince Edward Island), Workers' Compensation, hours of work laws, and Unemployment Insurance.[72]

In addition, Canada viewed British women as highly desirable immigrants and actively recruited domestics through official campaigns that touted specific economic and political rewards for European applicants. Conversely, the Caribbean was actively discouraged from sending its citizens. Canada's position of no recruitment, no special immigration schemes, and no government compromises regarding the Caribbean continued until 1973, when immigration policy regarding domestic workers underwent another shift.[73] Canada instituted increasingly restrictive guidelines regarding citizenship rights and occupational mobility.

This new immigration policy was to be built upon the existing framework that placed domestic workers in an exploitative relationship with their employers and that elevated the social and economic status of British domestics above that of Caribbean domestic workers. This system was the outcome of several policy decisions with respect to domestic workers that were made during the 1950s and 1960s and were premised on well-entrenched popular conceptions about the value of domestic labour and racist stereotypes about blacks.

Although the Unemployment Insurance plan's coverage was not universal during the 1950s, the decision to exclude domestic workers was based on two arguments. Bureaucrats stated that regulating what went on in private homes would be difficult, if not impossible. This in turn made determining who should rightfully be categorized as a domestic problematic. Bureaucrats also argued that Canada's traditionally high demand for domestic workers meant that domestics did not need Unemployment Insurance protection.[74] This decision served to legitimate the existing stereotypes about the cultural invisibility and economic insignificance of domestic labour. This in turn meant that even when the program was enlarged in the 1960s to cover most workers in the paid workforce, domestic workers continued to be excluded from coverage because of "the structural difficulties inherent in the occupation."[75]

Female employers were not isolated from this decision. Throughout the 1950s, many employers, aware of the negative effects of such a policy on their own status, actively discouraged officials from including domestic workers in the plan. Enlarging the scope of the Unemployment Insurance plan to encompass the private sphere meant that domestics would be protected from abuse since they could change employers or move into another area of work.[76] It also meant that more domestics would have to be imported as the demand would remain high. Both of these effects were not in the interests of the Canadian State. The exclusion of domestics from Unemployment Insurance affected Caribbean domestics more adversely than British women who, overwhelmingly, entered Canada as professional care givers under the new point system.[77]

Caribbean women also tended to be subject to exploitative conditions of work that were tolerated by the federal government – a fifty-four hour work week at a rate of eighty dollars a week was not uncommon. Although domestics were not forced to live in their employer's home, most of them did.[78] Caribbean domestic workers, seeking entrance into Canada at any cost and viewing employment in domestic work as a temporary state, rarely complained to immigration officials about the exploitation they endured as a result of the live-in component of this type of employment.[79] These women's need to acquire Canadian citizenship, which in turn would enable them to access more lucrative occupations, meant that Caribbean women were not likely to challenge their female employers who held the balance of power over their future status.

Caribbean women were not desired as members of the Canadian community and were seen as potential liabilities. Racist stereotypes about black women's promiscuity and about their rights to participate in the Canadian economic structure meant that Caribbean women were subject to various bureaucratic mechanisms designed to keep them from acquiring citizenship status. This in turn meant that they were unable to become part of the community of citizens who were able to make entitlement claims. As a memorandum to the Director of the Department of Citizenship and Immigration stated in 1966:

> You directed that the following action was to be taken: that the memorandum of March 18, 1966... be amended to include domestics in the list of occupations identified with an asterisk. *Occupations identified with an asterisk are specifically excluded for selection purposes.*[80]

Not only were Caribbean women excluded from the purview of the neutral immigration criteria, but the criterion of personal suitability allowed for subjective evaluations of a potential applicant. This was often used to restrict Caribbean women's access. As a 1968 memorandum to the Regional Director stated, "[We] have also refused, without interview, no less than 23 applicants where the applicants were unwed mothers with minor children... I can see no other way but to use discretionary action...".[81]

Furthermore, racial stereotypes about black women's sexual promiscuity and immorality meant that they were subjected to various arbitrary procedures. For example, Caribbean women who arrived in Canada as domestic workers were required to undergo compulsory medical examinations and those who wished to sponsor their fiancés had to hand over their private correspondences to Immigration officials in order to prove that the men they were sponsoring were in fact their fiancés and not impostors. These women were further required to say their vows within thirty days of their fiancés' arrival, or else the men would be deported.[82]

Thus, although the new immigration laws were universal in theory, in practice they were racially biased. The Canadian government instituted regulations that could curb the entry of black domestic workers to Canada, while simultaneously attempting to attract British women who were preferred as members of the national community. Caribbean women continued to enter Canada in order to work in private homes, but under increasingly restrictive conditions. Once here, they were expected by immigration officials and employers to work in service for a pre-determined period of time[83], thus serving the employers' interests. While Caribbean women were undergoing a process that would culminate in a wholesale curtailment of their citizenship rights, Canadian women were mobilizing to access their formal-legal rights and increase the entitlements that they could claim as citizens.

V. Canadian Women Mobilizing for Change

In the years between the two world wars, some of the women's groups established during the first wave of the women's movement, such as the National Council of Women in Canada (1893), the YWCA (1894), and the Canadian Federation of University Women (1919), continued to expand their support base and strengthen their organizations' power. These women's organizations, in conjunction with the Canadian Federation of Business and Professional Women's Clubs (1930), continued to advocate many of the social reforms they had sought throughout the previous period.[84]

Some middle class women's organizations continued in their reform efforts. However, without a motivating goal that could provide a focus for their activities as the demand for suffrage had, each group tended to work on its own specific issues, decided upon by the group's membership. Activities continued to be class biased. For example, the Canadian Federation of Business and Professional Women's Clubs, concentrating on the problems of women working in white collar sectors, requested that any legislation that might be introduced for workers in this sector apply equally to men and women.[85]

Throughout the 1940s and 1950s, maternal feminism thrived. The perception that women belonged in the private sphere and that there were basic differences between the genders dominated within society. The same middle class women's organizations that had adopted maternal feminism during the first wave of the movement actively supported these ideas.[86] Once the war was over and the economy was on the upswing, society pressured middle class women in particular to conform to this perception. The prevailing ideology dictated that they purchase goods for their households while continuing to provide their families with the material and intangible goods traditionally associated with women.[87]

Despite the fact that this ideology dominated society during the 1950s, the number of women finishing high school, going on to university and entering professional programs was increasing.[88] By 1960, many women were attending colleges and universities. This was possible as a result of new State policies concerning Canada's educational system. Universities had expanded, tuition fees were relatively inexpensive, and student loans and grants were accessible to those who did not come from typically educated and wealthy backgrounds.[89] As a result, women increasingly entered the public sphere, including middle class wives and mothers.[90]

By 1961, 29.3% of women and 18.5% of married women worked in the paid labour force compared to 24.5% and 9.6% in 1951.[91] Although more women were entering the paid work force, they continued to be relegated to less prestigious professions and to earn less than men – in 1961 Canadian women workers averaged $2 051 compared to the male average of $4 178. During this same year, only 7.7% of working women were remunerated on par with men.[92]

During the 1960s, women of all backgrounds, encountering this fundamentally inequitable social structure, began to mobilize for change. Working class women organized from within working class organizations; middle class women continued to mobilize through their established organizations; and some women began to organize through liberation movements. By 1966, the women's movement had made its presence known on the Canadian political landscape. The women's liberation, feminist, and women's rights groups had emerged as distinct strands of the movement.[93]

Student activism led to the formation of women's liberation groups. The women belonging to this branch of the women's movement tended to be young, middle class, and adherents of left wing ideology. These women used theories of oppression to analyze their own lives and soon founded women's liberation groups in cities across the country. However, as theories of oppression developed, women became divided over analyses and regrouped into different ideological factions.[94]

Some women adhered to the Marx–Engels analysis that presented capitalism as the main force of oppression. These women believed that women's oppression was not a fundamental, universal, or biological given but the result of a social structure that retained the family as its base. They argued that once subsistence–level farming was eliminated as a form of social organization, families were able to accumulate surplus. This separation of direct producers from the means of production resulted in the formation of a class society that coincided with the oppression of women. Women were forced to stay home and take care of domestic and reproductive functions while men worked outside of the home to create sustainable surplus. Consequently, these women also argued that the first class division was between men and women. With the inception of capitalism, women were placed at a greater disadvantage since men were able to improve their status by means of women's unpaid domestic labour. These women argued that the abolition of capitalism would mean the end of women's oppression, as there would be no distinction between use–value and surplus–value labour: men's and women's labour would be equally valued.[95] These women tended to organize outside of established women's organizations.

The second group to emerge was that of the feminists, who believed that women's oppression was a fundamental and universal feature of all societies. They attributed women's oppression to male–dominated societies wherein social and economic roles are ascribed on the basis of the gender to which one belongs. Women were ensured a subordinate status since women's roles were valued less than men's.[96] The feminists believed that women's oppression could not be eradicated by granting them a larger slice of the social pie, stating, "We believe that the pie itself is rotten."[97] Women would only be emancipated once the sexual division of labour was eliminated and society valued men and women equally as human beings, thereby providing members of each group with equal opportunities for self-actualization not bound up with traditional sex–role stereotypes. For them, the struggle from within the system was ineffectual. Thus, both women's liberation and feminist groups tended to operate at the grassroots level and outside of established political institutions.[98]

Women's rights groups grew out of the women's organizations of the first wave. The women who belonged to these groups tended to be white middle class married women. They did not question the traditional division of spheres. Instead, they fell squarely within the liberal feminist tradition. Seeking legislative solutions to concerns such as discrimination in the workplace, wage parity and property laws, they tended to adopt views associated with equality of individuals.[99] Women's subordinate position was perceived to be the result of exclusion from the social pie. Gender equality could be achieved by giving women access to a greater piece of that pie.

Women's rights groups were oblivious to issues of race and class. They tended to ignore the situation of working women who were frequently employed in industries that were neither mechanized nor automated and which therefore paid lower wages. Within these industries, profits are dependent on cheap labour. Women's rights groups promoted individualistic solutions that were largely irrelevant to most working women's reality, such as increasing the number of women in the upper echelons of industry and the professions.[100] This was especially true for black women who tended to be concentrated in the lowest rungs of the socioeconomic hierarchy and had little opportunity to access these more lucrative employment occupations. Yet, adhering to a strategy of working from within, and claiming to be the voice of the women's movement, these middle class women subsequently came to dominate the women's movement.

Women's rights groups came to be involved in an intimate relationship with the federal government, beginning with the creation of the Voice of Women on July 28, 1960. The following

September, the organization set up a national office in Toronto. Middle class women, many of whom were mothers, formed the Voice of Women in the hopes of helping to prevent the threat of nuclear war. The organization primarily recruited women and by the autumn of 1961 it boasted a membership of 5 000. Until 1963, the government and the media treated the Voice of Women with the respect that had traditionally been given to maternal causes. At this juncture, the Pearson government changed its policy concerning nuclear weapons, thereby enabling Bomarc missiles to be placed on Canadian soil. The Voice of Women criticized this decision.[101]

After this incident, the organization expanded and continued to attack the government and individual MPs for specific policies. As a result, Ottawa no longer treated The Voice of Women as a preferred group, telling them that, "These decisions are made by our political masters. The politicians are responsible to the voters."[102] Many of these women subsequently decided to enter the political sphere with the aim of acquiring the power to change policies, and came to support the idea of a royal commission on the status of women.[103]

In 1963 the United Nations marked 1968 as the International Year of Human Rights, thereby sparking the idea of a royal commission on the status of women among women's rights groups. The United Nations highlighted this year in an effort to urge all nations to grant all their citizens full human rights. Women's rights groups saw this landmark event as an opportunity to set up a royal commission that would investigate their concerns and make them known to the government.[104] The State was seen by these women as a benevolent body that could and would redress systemic inequalities that had traditionally prevented women from participating in the political and economic spheres of the nation.[105] None of these women adhered to the radical or Marxist perspective. They accepted the class system and the notion that women were responsible for domestic work. They merely wanted the government to implement mechanisms that would allow them access to the employment opportunities they had been led to believe were viable options.[106]

On April 18, 1966, Laura Sabia, president of the Canadian Federation of University Women, invited all members of long-standing women's organizations to a meeting.[107] On May 3, 1966 the women met in Toronto in order to discuss taking collective action regarding women's status. Fifty women, acting as ambassadors for thirty-two women's groups, and the press participated in the proceedings. The end result was a steering committee composed of nine women and led by Sabia. On May 27, 1966, this steering committee decided to urge the involved groups to lobby the government for the establishment of a royal commission.[108]

Upon meeting for a second time, the steering committee decided to create a new organization that would focus on improving women's status. This organization, called the Committee on the Equality of Women in Canada, had a mandate to pressure the government to set up a royal commission on the status of women.[109] The Committee on the Equality of Women in Canada considered a royal commission on the status of women as the most effective means of bringing the issue of sexual discrimination to the nation's attention. This committee believed that a royal commission on the status of women was the most effective vehicle for making the needs and wants of individual women as well as groups (issues that were politically sensitive within the context of the International Year of Human Rights) known to the State.[110]

On November 19, 1966 the Committee on the Equality of Women in Canada presented the Canadian government with a petition demanding the establishment of a royal commission on the status of women. The purpose of the body would be "to inquire into, to report on and to make recommendations which will enable women to achieve such excellence in public and private life as meets the standards set by the Universal Declaration of Human Rights....".[111] Although the petition represented two million Canadian women, each of whom belonged to a national women's organization, the government was not very receptive to the proposal. It was only after the November presentation that two events tipped the balance in women's favor.[112]

Women in the House of Commons supported the position

advanced by the Committee on the Equality of Women in Canada. For many years, Secretary of State Judy LaMarsh, the only female cabinet minister, had been demanding the establishment of a royal commission on the status of women and backed the decision reached at the November 19 meeting. During this period, she communicated frequently with Sabia as each, respectively, took on the role of internal and external advocacy. Grace MacInnis, the only other female member of parliament, also pressed for the creation of the commission.[113]

The second factor that influenced the government to favour the formation of a royal commission was the support the news media gave to the demands of the Committee for the Equality of Women in Canada. The July issue of Chatelaine ran an editorial demanding that a royal commission on the status of women be set up.[114] On January 5, 1967, an article appeared on the front page of the Toronto Globe and Mail entitled, "Women's March may back call for Rights Probe". This news story was a factor that heavily influenced the government's decision. On February 5, 1967, the Pearson government stated that it would create a royal commission to examine the status of women, thereby lending legitimacy to the notion of women's subordinate status as a social problem. Ultimately, women's concerns were acknowledged as a legitimate political issue and the Royal Commission on the Status of Women was created because well-established women's groups, drawing on their previously entrenched maternal clout, made their demands through acceptable channels.[115]

The Commission was headed by Anne Francis, and from 1967 to 1969 its members listened to briefs, held forums so that women could articulate the problems they encountered, and provided a focus for the activites of the women's movement.[116] During this period, the women's movement was expanding at a rapid rate and two distinct groups emerged: grassroots feminists and institutionalized feminists.[117]

At the grassroots level, groups formed and disbanded on an impromptu basis. Women worked in collectives and in non-hierarchical organizations.[118] Some focused on one problem. Others embraced a host of problems while engaging in in-depth analy-

sis. Most grassroots feminists groups were locally-based, concentrating on raising awareness and reaching out to their sisters in
need by providing necessary services. These women tended to be
unaware of and uninterested in the institutional processes necessary to attain the goals of their movement. As such, grassroots
feminists came to occupy a peripheral position in the political
process.[119]

Liberal middle class feminists, on the other hand, came to
focus all of their attention on the Royal Commission on the
Status of Women. In January 1971, Sabia rallied the Committee on
the Equality of Women in Canada, stating, "only in joint *action* can
we be sure that the Report will not gather dust on some
Parliamentary shelf."[120] The decision was thus taken to reorganize
the Committee on the Equality of Women into the National ad
hoc Action Committee on the Status of Women. This organization's mandate was to pressure the government into following
the recommendations of the Royal Commission. In 1972 the
group relinquished its 'ad hoc' definition, becoming the National
Action Committee on the Status of Women. Institutionalized
middle class women's organizations, many of which had been
established during the first wave of the movement, were the
primary member groups involved in this organization. As such,
policy-makers and the public came to view the National Action
Committee on the Status of Women as the voice of the women's
movement.[121]

Although the Royal Commission, in its 167 recommendations,
endorsed some far-reaching changes to the social structure, such
as universal and nationalized day care, the government was not
bound to comply with nor implement them. The National Action
Committee was forced into the position of a lobby group that
had power only insofar as it could induce the government to
comply with its demands. Given the limitations of its organizational resources and power, as a lobby group it could only act in
response to government policies and proposed legislation. These
policies tended to be of a more conservative nature and were
framed within the discourse of equality of opportunity.

The government, acting in accordance with the ideology of the

Keynesian Welfare State and its assumptions of traditional familial structures and the proper gender order, was to ignore the
more radical (and costly) recommendations that the Commission
had issued. The National Action Committee in turn, being primarily a middle class women's organization, focused on the
issues its membership perceived to be the most salient; that is,
middle class women's concerns. Through this process, nationalized day care came to occupy a lesser position on the organization's scale of priorities. Moreover, in the early years, many of the
issues that came to dominate the organization's agenda – abortion, the elimination of sexual discrimination in the workplace
and education – did not take into consideration the mediating
factors of race and class. This effectively limited the potential for
a unified women's movement that could effect radical change in
the social order. Women came to be included in Canada's public
sphere, but some women were included more than others.

VI. Summing It Up:
Included on Conditional Terms

During the period examined, several changes occurred in
Canadian women's citizenship status. The Canadian government,
by implementing the Royal Commission on the Status of Women,
acknowledged that women's inclusion in the public sphere was
constrained by existing social, economic, and political arrangements. The government, recognizing Canadian women's subordinate status as a legitimate social problem, enabled Canadian
women to increase the entitlement claims they could make as
citizens. Yet the entitlements that they could claim fell within
strict parameters – those defined by the Keynesian Welfare State.
These entitlements were geared toward enabling women to enter
politics and the economy on a more equal footing, but, with the
exception of a brief mention of daycare and maternity leave, they
in no way challenged the organization of domestic labour.

Domestic labour remained women's responsibility and, conceptually, remained invisible in both its importance and extent. Moreover, because liberal middle class feminists' conception was the dominant force pressing the State for change, the entitlements subsequently established did not differentiate between classes; they were to apply equally to all women. Ironically, the entitlements would serve to privilege some women more than others, in particular white middle and upper class women. Because the State continued to treat domestic labour as a personal rather than a social and economic need[122], it was largely only white middle and upper class women who could afford to hire replacement home workers and make full use of their entitlements.

Although Canadian women gained increased rights during this period, domestic workers' rights were concurrently curtailed. Changes in immigration policy regarding domestic workers were distinctive on two fronts. They allowed racial groups formerly excluded from Canada to enter the country, while simultaneously curtailing the citizenship rights that these groups could expect. This shift is most notable with the inclusion of black women from the Caribbean. Domestic workers from the Caribbean were placed in an unregulated market where they were denied post-war welfare measures such as Unemployment Insurance that would protect them against exploitation. The terms governing the working conditions of these women created an inequitable set of relations whereby Canadian white middle and upper class women's status was enhanced by the bonded labour of those who did not possess citizenship status. This set of relations was possible due to the poverty of the Caribbean source nations and Caribbean women's desire to attain citizenship status. In this process, however, the entitlements associated with citizenship came to be social goods that had to be earned. For black women, cast as undesirable citizens, this meant a period of indentureship in domestic labour.

Notes

1. Janine Brodie, *Politics on the Margins: Restructuring and the Canadian Women's Movement* (Nova Scotia: Fernwood Publishing Company, 1995), 39.

2. Kathleen B. Jones, "Citizenship in a Woman-Friendly Polity," *Signs: Journal of Women in Culture and Society* 15 (1990), 805.

3. Janine Brodie, *Politics on the Margins: Restructuring and the Canadian Women's Movement* (Nova Scotia: Fernwood Publishing Company, 1995), 13, 15, 39.

4. *Ibid.*, 15.

5. *Ibid.*, 39–41. Janine Brodie, *Politics on the Boundaries: Restructuring and the Canadian Women's Movement* (Toronto: Robarts Center for Canadian Studies, 1994), 28.

6. Nancy Fraser, "Talking About Needs: Interpretive Contests as Political Conflicts in Welfare-State Societies," *Ethics* 99 (January 1989), 300.

7. Janine Brodie, *Politics on the Margins: Restructuring and the Canadian Women's Movement* (Nova Scotia: Fernwood Publishing Company, 1995), 40-1. Janine Brodie, *Politics on the Boundaries: Restructuring and the Canadian Women's Movement* (Toronto: Robarts Center for Canadian Studies, 1994), 29.

8. Janine Brodie, *Politics on the Margins: Restructuring and the Canadian Women's Movement* (Nova Scotia: Fernwood Publishing Company, 1995), 43.

9. Sylvia Bashevkin, "Independence Versus Partisanship: Dilemmas in the Political History of Women in English Canada," *Rethinking Canada: The Promise of Women's History*, eds. Veronica Strong-Boag and Anita Clair Fellman (Toronto: Copp Clark Pitman Ltd., 1991), 430-1.

10. Agnes Calliste, "Race, Gender and Canadian Immigration Policy: Blacks from the Caribbean, 1900-1932," *Journal of Canadian Studies* 28 (Winter 1993-1994), 145.

11. Rina Cohen, "A Brief History of Racism in Immigration Policies for Recruiting Domestics," *Canadian Women Studies* 14 (1994), 83.
12. *Ibid.*
13. Dionne Brand, "We Weren't Allowed to Go into Factory Work Until Hitler Started the War: The 1920s to the 1940s," *We are Rooted Here and They Can't Pull Us Up: Essays in African Canadian Women's History*, ed. Peggy Bristow (Toronto: University of Toronto Press, 1994), 175, 178, 181.
14. Jane Errington, "Pioneers and Suffragists," *Changing Patterns: Women in Canada*, eds. Sandra Burt, Lorraine Code and Lindsay Dorney (Toronto: McClelland & Stewart, 1990), 75-6.
15. Sylvia Bashevkin, "Independence Versus Partisanship: Dilemmas in the Political History of Women in English Canada," *Rethinking Canada: The Promise of Women's History*, eds. Veronica Strong-Boag and Anita Clair Fellman (Toronto: Copp Clark Pitman Ltd., 1991), 432.
16. Jane Errington, "Pioneers and Suffragists," *Changing Patterns: Women in Canada* eds. Sandra Burt, Lorraine Code and Lindsay Dorney (Toronto: McClelland & Stewart, 1990), 76.
17. Dionne Brand, "We Weren't Allowed to Go into Factory Work Until Hitler Started the War: The 1920s to the 1940s," *We are Rooted Here and They Can't Pull Us Up: Essays in African Canadian Women's History*, ed. Peggy Bristow (Toronto: University of Toronto Press, 1994), 179, 181.
18. Jane Errington, "Pioneers and Suffragists," *Changing Patterns: Women in Canada*, eds. Sandra Burt, Lorraine Code and Lindsay Dorney (Toronto: McClelland & Stewart, 1990), 76.
19. Sandra Burt, "The Women's Movement: Working to Transform Public Life," *The Women's Movement: Working to Transform Public Life*, eds. James P. Bickerton and Alain G. Gagnon (Ontario: Broadview Press, 1994), 212.
20. Sylvia Bashevkin, "Independence Versus Partisanship: Dilemmas in the Political History of Women in English Canada," *Rethinking Canada: The Promise of Women's History*, eds. Veronica Strong-Boag and Anita Clair Fellman (Toronto: Copp Clark Pitman Ltd., 1991), 432.
21. Rina Cohen, "A Brief History of Racism in Immigration Policies for Recruiting Domestics," *Canadian Women Studies* 14 (1994), 83.
22. Patricia Daenzer, *Regulating Class Privilege: Immigrant Servants in Canada, 1940s-1990s* (Toronto: Canadian Scholars Press, 1993), 21-2.

23. Director of the Department of Citizenship and Immigration, quoted in *ibid.*, 34.

24. Lynne Teather, "The Feminist Mosaic," *Women in the Canadian Mosaic*, ed. Gwen Matheson (Toronto: Peter Martin Associates Limited, 1976), 312.

25. Sylvia Bashevkin, "Independence Versus Partisanship: Dilemmas in the Political History of Women in English Canada," *Rethinking Canada: The Promise of Women's History*, eds. Veronica Strong-Boag and Anita Clair Fellman (Toronto: Copp Clark Pitman Ltd., 1991), 432.

26. Sandra Burt, "The Women's Movement: Working to Transform Public Life," *The Women's Movement: Working to Transform Public Life*, eds. James P. Bickerton and Alain G. Gagnon (Ontario: Broadview Press, 1994), 212.

27. Patricia Daenzer, *Regulating Class Privilege: Immigrant Servants in Canada, 1940s-1990s* (Toronto: Canadian Scholars Press, 1993), 23.

28. Rina Cohen, "A Brief History of Racism in Immigration Policies for Recruiting Domestics," *Canadian Women Studies* 14 (1994), 83.

29. Patricia Daenzer, *Regulating Class Privilege: Immigrant Servants in Canada, 1940s-1990s* (Toronto: Canadian Scholars Press, 1993), 23.

30. Linda Carty, "African Canadian Women and the State: Labour Only Please," *We Are Rooted Here and They Can't Pull Us Up: Essays in African Canadian Women's History* ed. Peggy Bristow (Toronto: University of Toronto Press, 1994), 214.

31. Patricia Daenzer, *Regulating Class Privilege: Immigrant Servants in Canada, 1940s-1990s* (Toronto: Canadian Scholars Press, 1993), 23-4. Ruth Lynette Harris, *The Transformation of Canadian Policies and Programs to Recruit Foreign Labour: The Case of Caribbean Female Domestic Workers, 1950-1990s* (Ph.D. Dissertation: Michigan State University, 1988), 72, 76, 79.

32. Patricia Daenzer, *Regulating Class Privilege: Immigrant Servants in Canada, 1940s-1990s* (Toronto: Canadian Scholars Press, 1993), 23-4, 26.

33. *Ibid.*, 26.

34 *Ibid.*, 26-8

35. *Ibid.*, 25, 27-8.

36. *Ibid.*, 29.

37. *Ibid.*, 8, 29-30, 50.

38. *Ibid.*, 50-1.

39. *Ibid.*, 43.

40. *Ibid.*, 43-4, 49.

41. Lynne Teather, "The Feminist Mosaic," *Women in the Canadian Mosaic,* ed. Gwen Matheson (Toronto: Peter Martin Associates Limited, 1976), 314.

42. Alice James, "Poverty: Canada's Legacy to Women," *Women Unite: An Anthology of the Canadian Women's Movement* (Toronto: Canadian Women's Educational Press, 1972), 126.

43. *Ibid.*, 130.

44. Ruth Lynette Harris, *The Transformation of Canadian Policies and Programs to Recruit Foreign Labour: The Case of Caribbean Female Domestic Workers, 1950-1990s* (Ph.D. Dissertation: Michigan State University, 1988), 78.

45. Vic Satzewich, "Racism and Canadian Immigration Policy: The Government's View of Caribbean Migration, 1962–1966," *Canadian Ethnic Studies* 21 (1989), 91. Ruth Lynette Harris, *The Transformation of Canadian Policies and Programs to Recruit Foreign Labour: The Case of Caribbean Female Domestic Workers, 1950-1990s* (Ph.D. Dissertation: Michigan State University, 1988), 76.

46. Ruth Lynette Harris, *The Transformation of Canadian Policies and Programs to Recruit Foreign Labour: The Case of Caribbean Female Domestic Workers, 1950-1990s* (Ph.D. Dissertation: Michigan State University, 1988), 76, 78. Up until 1955 the only way blacks could enter Canada as potential permanent immigrants was "as (1) sponsored close relatives of Canadian citizens, (2) as unsponsored individuals of exceptional merit (i.e., humanitarian reasons or as potentially outstanding Canadian citizens), and (3) as employer–sponsored special group movements of labour, such as farm workers, nurses or domestics, which were bilateral government sanctioned work schemes". Ruth Lynette Harris, *The Transformation of Canadian Policies and Programs to Recruit Foreign Labour: The Case of Caribbean Female Domestic Workers, 1950-1990s* (Ph.D. Dissertation: Michigan State University, 1988), 71-2.

47. Patricia Daenzer, *Regulating Class Privilege: Immigrant Servants in Canada, 1940s-1990s* (Toronto: Canadian Scholars Press, 1993), 53.

48. Ruth Lynette Harris, *The Transformation of Canadian Policies and Programs to Recruit Foreign Labour: The Case of Caribbean Female Domestic Workers, 1950-1990s* (Ph.D. Dissertation: Michigan State University, 1988), 72, 79, 189.

49. Canada had a number of economic interests in the region, most of

which were structured so as to be vertically integrated. These included "trade, extractive industries, small manufacturers, banking and insurance, transportation and public utilities and tourism". Ruth Lynette Harris, *The Transformation of Canadian Policies and Programs to Recruit Foreign Labour: The Case of Caribbean Female Domestic Workers, 1950-1990s* (Ph.D. Dissertation: Michigan State University, 1988), 132.

50. Ruth Lynette Harris, *The Transformation of Canadian Policies and Programs to Recruit Foreign Labour: The Case of Caribbean Female Domestic Workers, 1950-1990s* (Ph.D. Dissertation: Michigan State University, 1988), 83, 86.

51. Department of Citizenship and Immigration, Department of Labour, quoted in *ibid.*, 81.

52. *Ibid.*, 80-1, 89, 96. Patricia Daenzer, *Regulating Class Privilege: Immigrant Servants in Canada, 1940s-1990s* (Toronto: Canadian Scholars Press, 1993), 54.

53. Ruth Lynette Harris, *The Transformation of Canadian Policies and Programs to Recruit Foreign Labour: The Case of Caribbean Female Domestic Workers, 1950-1990s* (Ph.D. Dissertation: Michigan State University, 1988), 89, 94.

54. Patricia Daenzer, *Regulating Class Privilege: Immigrant Servants in Canada, 1940s-1990s* (Toronto: Canadian Scholars Press, 1993), 54.

55. Ruth Lynette Harris, *The Transformation of Canadian Policies and Programs to Recruit Foreign Labour: The Case of Caribbean Female Domestic Workers, 1950-1990s* (Ph.D. Dissertation: Michigan State University, 1988), 96.

56. Patricia Daenzer, *Regulating Class Privilege: Immigrant Servants in Canada, 1940s-1990s* (Toronto: Canadian Scholars Press, 1993), 69.

57. Ruth Lynette Harris, *The Transformation of Canadian Policies and Programs to Recruit Foreign Labour: The Case of Caribbean Female Domestic Workers, 1950-1990s* (Ph.D. Dissertation: Michigan State University, 1988), 90.

58. *Ibid.*, 99, 134, 137.

59. *Ibid.*, 101.

60. Deputy Minister, quoted in Patricia Daenzer, *Regulating Class Privilege: Immigrant Servants in Canada, 1940s-1990s* (Toronto: Canadian Scholars Press, 1993), 82.

61. *Ibid.*, 66.

62. *Ibid.*

63. Vic Satzewich, "Racism and Canadian Immigration Policy: The

Government's View of Caribbean Migration, 1962–1966," *Canadian Ethnic Studies* 21 (1989), 78.

64. Agnes Calliste, "Canada's Immigration Policy and Domestics from the Caribbean: The Second Domestic Scheme," *Race, Class and Gender: Bonds and Barriers*, ed. Jesse Vorste (Toronto: Garamond Press, 1991), 150.

65. Patricia Daenzer, *Regulating Class Privilege: Immigrant Servants in Canada, 1940s-1990s* (Toronto: Canadian Scholars Press, 1993), 74–5.

66. *Ibid.*, 75.

67. *Ibid.*

68. *Ibid.*, 76

69. *Ibid.* Ruth Lynette Harris, *The Transformation of Canadian Policies and Programs to Recruit Foreign Labour: The Case of Caribbean Female Domestic Workers, 1950-1990s* (Ph.D. Dissertation: Michigan State University, 1988), 144.

70. Ruth Lynette Harris, *The Transformation of Canadian Policies and Programs to Recruit Foreign Labour: The Case of Caribbean Female Domestic Workers, 1950-1990s* (Ph.D. Dissertation: Michigan State University, 1988), 147.

71. *Ibid.*

72. Patricia Daenzer, *Regulating Class Privilege: Immigrant Servants in Canada, 1940s-1990s* (Toronto: Canadian Scholars Press, 1993), 67, 69–70.

73. Ruth Lynette Harris, *The Transformation of Canadian Policies and Programs to Recruit Foreign Labour: The Case of Caribbean Female Domestic Workers, 1950-1990s* (Ph.D. Dissertation: Michigan State University, 1988), 139–40, 152, 155.

74. Patricia Daenzer, *Regulating Class Privilege: Immigrant Servants in Canada, 1940s-1990s* (Toronto: Canadian Scholars Press, 1993), 48–9, 55.

75. *Ibid.*, 55.

76. *Ibid.*, 67.

77. *Ibid.*, 76.

78. *Ibid.*, 69.

79. Ruth Lynette Harris, *The Transformation of Canadian Policies and Programs to Recruit Foreign Labour: The Case of Caribbean Female Domestic Workers, 1950-1990s* (Ph.D. Dissertation: Michigan State University, 1988), 147, 150.

80. Quoted in Patricia Daenzer, *Regulating Class Privilege: Immigrant Servants in Canada, 1940s-1990s* (Toronto: Canadian Scholars Press, 1993), 84.

81. Quoted in *ibid.*

82. Vic Satzewich, "Racism and Canadian Immigration Policy: The Government's View of Caribbean Migration, 1962–1966," *Canadian Ethnic Studies* 21 (1989), 91–2.

83. Patricia Daenzer, *Regulating Class Privilege: Immigrant Servants in Canada, 1940s-1990s* (Toronto: Canadian Scholars Press, 1993), 77.

84. Sylvia Bashevkin, "Independence Versus Partisanship: Dilemmas in the Political History of Women in English Canada," *Rethinking Canada: The Promise of Women's History*, eds. Veronica Strong–Boag and Anita Clair Fellman (Toronto: Copp Clark Pitman Ltd., 1991), 431.

85. Lynne Teather, "The Feminist Mosaic," *Women in the Canadian Mosaic*, ed. Gwen Matheson (Toronto: Peter Martin Associates Limited, 1976), 308–10.

86. Jane Errington, "Pioneers and Suffragists," *Changing Patterns: Women in Canada*, eds. Sandra Burt, Lorraine Code and Lindsay Dorney (Toronto: McClelland & Stewart, 1990), 76.

87. Sylvia Bashevkin, "Independence Versus Partisanship: Dilemmas in the Political History of Women in English Canada," *Rethinking Canada: The Promise of Women's History*, eds. Veronica Strong–Boag and Anita Clair Fellman (Toronto: Copp Clark Pitman Ltd., 1991), 432.

88. Jane Errington, "Pioneers and Suffragists," *Changing Patterns: Women in Canada*, eds. Sandra Burt, Lorraine Code and Lindsay Dorney (Toronto: McClelland & Stewart, 1990), 76.

89. Nancy Adamson, Linda Briskin and Margaret McPhail, *Feminists Organizing for Change: The Contemporary Women's Movement in Canada* (Toronto: Oxford University Press, 1988), 38.

90. Jane Errington, "Pioneers and Suffragists," *Changing Patterns: Women in Canada*, eds. Sandra Burt, Lorraine Code and Lindsay Dorney (Toronto: McClelland & Stewart, 1990), 76.

91. Alice James, "Poverty: Canada's Legacy to Women," *Women Unite: An Anthology of the Canadian Women's Movement* (Toronto: Canadian Women's Educational Press, 1972), 126. Lynne Teather, "The Feminist Mosaic," *Women in the Canadian Mosaic*, ed. Gwen Matheson (Toronto: Peter Martin Associates Limited, 1976), 314.

92. Alice James, "Poverty: Canada's Legacy to Women," *Women Unite: An Anthology of the Canadian Women's Movement* (Toronto: Canadian Women's Educational Press, 1972), 137.

93. Lynne Teather, "The Feminist Mosaic," *Women in the Canadian Mosaic*,

ed. Gwen Matheson (Toronto: Peter Martin Associates Limited, 1976), 316.

94. *Ibid.*, 321.

95. For an interesting discussion about the role of capitalism and the family in structuring women's subordinate status see Peggy Morton, "Women's Work is Never Done... Or the Production, Maintenance and Reproduction of Labour Power," *Women Unite: An Anthology of the Canadian Women's Movement* (Toronto: Canadian Women's Educational Press, 1972), 46–68. See also Judy Berstein, Peggy Morton, Linda Seese and Myrna Wood, "Sisters, Brothers, Lovers... Listen...," *Women Unite: An Anthology of the Canadian Women's Movement* (Toronto: Canadian Women's Educational Press, 1972), 31–39.

96. Lynne Teather, "The Feminist Mosaic," *Women in the Canadian Mosaic*, ed. Gwen Matheson (Toronto: Peter Martin Associates Limited, 1976), 322.

97. Bonnie Kreps, "Radical Feminism 1," *Women Unite: An Anthology of the Canadian Women's Movement* (Toronto: Canadian Women's Educational Press, 1972), 75.

98. Nancy Adamson, Linda Briskin and Margaret McPhail, *Feminists Organizing for Change: The Contemporary Women's Movement in Canada* (Toronto: Oxford University Press, 1988), 51.

99. Lynne Teather, "The Feminist Mosaic," *Women in the Canadian Mosaic*, ed. Gwen Matheson (Toronto: Peter Martin Associates Limited, 1976), 317.

100. Jean Rands, "Towards an Organization of Working Women," *Women Unite: An Anthology of the Canadian Women's Movement* (Toronto: Canadian Women's Educational Press, 1972), 144–5.

101. Kay Macpherson and Meg Sears, "The Voice of Women: A History," *Women in the Canadian Mosaic*, ed. Gwen Matheson (Toronto: Peter Martin Associates Limited, 1976), 72–5.

102. Quoted in *ibid.*, 83.

103. *Ibid.*, 80–1, 83.

104. Lynne Teather, "The Feminist Mosaic," *Women in the Canadian Mosaic*, ed. Gwen Matheson (Toronto: Peter Martin Associates Limited, 1976), 316.

105. Janine Brodie, *Politics on the Margins: Restructuring and the Canadian Women's Movement* (Nova Scotia: Fernwood Publishing Company,

1995), 43.

106. Nancy Adamson, Linda Briskin and Margaret McPhail, *Feminists Organizing for Change: The Contemporary Women's Movement in Canada* (Toronto: Oxford University Press, 1988), 38.

107. Cerise Morris, "'Determination and Thoroughness': The Movement for a Royal Commission on the Status of Women in Canada," *Atlantis* 5 (1980), 10.

108. *Ibid.*

109. *Ibid.*, 11.

110. *Ibid.*, 11–2.

111. Quoted in *ibid.*, 13.

112. Lynne Teather, "The Feminist Mosaic," *Women in the Canadian Mosaic*, ed. Gwen Matheson (Toronto: Peter Martin Associates Limited, 1976), 317–8.

113. Cerise Morris, "'Determination and Thoroughness': The Movement for a Royal Commission on the Status of Women in Canada," *Atlantis* 5 (1980), 14.

114. *Ibid.*, 10.

115. *Ibid.*, 14, 15, 17, 19.

116. Lynne Teather, "The Feminist Mosaic," *Women in the Canadian Mosaic*, ed. Gwen Matheson (Toronto: Peter Martin Associates Limited, 1976), 318.

117. Nancy Adamson, Linda Briskin and Margaret McPhail, *Feminists Organizing for Change: The Contemporary Women's Movement in Canada* (Toronto: Oxford University Press, 1988), 29. Although these two terms will be used again throughout this text, for reasons of simplicity, they will not be cited again.

118. Lynne Teather, "The Feminist Mosaic," *Women in the Canadian Mosaic*, ed. Gwen Matheson (Toronto: Peter Martin Associates Limited, 1976), 324.

119. Nancy Adamson, Linda Briskin and Margaret McPhail, *Feminists Organizing for Change: The Contemporary Women's Movement in Canada* (Toronto: Oxford University Press, 1988), 8, 12, 54.

120. Laura Sabia, quoted in *ibid.*, 52.

121. *Ibid.*, 52–4.

122. Nancy Fraser, "Talking About Needs: Interpretive Contests as Political Conflicts in Welfare-State Societies," *Ethics* 99 (January 1989), 300.

Chapter 3

ONE STEP FORWARD, TWO STEPS BACK
The Issues of Nationalized Day Care and Foreign Domestic Workers Since the 1970s

With the creation of the Royal Commission on the Status of Women in 1967, the State formally recognized Canadian women's subordinate status as a social problem and women came to occupy a position of inclusion. With the release of the Commission's recommendations, the State conceded that the existing social, economic and political structures of Canadian society restricted women's freedom to exercise their citizenship rights. Although the Commission made several radical recommendations, such as creating State–funded child care centres available throughout the nation and increasing Mother's Allowances by one hundred percent, the government immediately rejected these proposals. The decision was not challenged by any of the involved groups.[1] This was a pattern to be repeated for all of the Commission's radical recommendations.

Although it was widely recognized that women had the right to be included in the public sphere, the State was unwilling to endorse any new policies, except those that fell squarely within the liberal tradition. These types of policies were, and continue to be, associated with the notion that women's rights can be equated with human rights. They aim to achieve gender equality through the lens of equality of opportunity; that is, by granting women the same rights as men. These rights are ensured through various legislation, such as equal pay for equal work and regulations barring discrimination in both the workplace and education. Liberals assume that once these barriers are removed, women will be able to compete on a level playing field for society's assets.[2] This type of policy treats women as a homogeneous group, and does not address the fact that white middle and upper women, because of their race and class, are more privileged than others and thus benefit more from these policies.

According to Trimble (1990), there are several problems inherent in these policies. Firmly rooted in the idea of separate spheres, they continue to value the public sphere more than the private. Although child tax credits provide some assistance to women, women continue to bear the brunt of domestic responsibilities. Thus women have to either reject their private role by remaining single or childless or make alternate arrangements for their private sphere duties in order to enter the public sphere on an equal footing with men. Otherwise, women are forced to work a double day. Those who have the option of hiring replacement homeworkers tend to be white middle and upper class women. This is possible due to State policies that have ensured a continuous and ample supply of third world women willing to work in domestic service under increasingly restrictive conditions for sub-minimum wages.

The State had several reasons for resisting the implementation of policies that would relieve women of their child care responsibilities and thus ensure greater gender equality. These corresponded to the State's decision to institute increasingly restrictive guidelines regarding domestic workers. The Keynesian Welfare State's basic premise, including its assumptions about citizen entitlements, was beginning to break down by the 1970s. At this juncture, the Canadian State began to modify its social policies in keeping with neoliberal ideas, which were born of the belief that the State does not have a responsibility towards its citizens in the form of an all–encompassing welfare plan. Rather, the State should allow the market's conditions to regulate the nation's economy and, hence, the distribution of goods. This neoliberal discourse attempts to decrease citizens' expectations of the State. It is accomplished by reducing the number of legitimate political claims in a new social and economic structure that places the market and the family's autonomy above all else.[3] A system of nationalized day care would increase the claims that women could make and would place a large fiscal burden on the State.

At the same time, the Canadian State managed to assuage some of the need for cheap child care workers by importing women from the third world to perform domestic labour without granting them citizenship rights. By denying the women citizenship rights, the State restricted the number of citizens able to make entitlement claims, while simultaneously enabling some of its citizens to exercise the rights that they had been granted. This policy was possible because of the global stratification that places some nations in an economically dependent position. Third world countries with underdeveloped economies remained dependent on migrant workers' remittances. Thus, they actively participated in the process by which women of colour from the third world, most notably the Caribbean and the Philippines, are encouraged to work at times in virtual captivity, as domestic workers for Canadian women.

The institutionalized women's movement in Canada facilitated these policies. The National Action Committee, acting as the voice of the women's movement and operating within the liberal feminist tradition, accepted the Royal Commission on the Status of Women's recommendations as a blueprint for change. The National Action Committee, composed primarily of white middle and upper class women, did not challenge domestic work's economic and cultural invisibility. Adhering to the view that increasing women's participation and representation would result in emancipation, the organization consistently refused to admit as members groups that advocated wages for housework. In effect, by adhering to this stance the National Action Committee unwittingly legitimated the low wages that non-immigrant women of colour working as domestics were receiving.

The National Action Committee, as a lobby group, focused on achieving legislative reforms in areas such as pay equity and abortion – measures that they viewed as helping all women attain parity with their male counterparts. However, since it was a lobby group, it operated on a reactive basis. The State influenced its agenda, thereby ensuring that its list of priorities was characterized by a more conservative nature.[4] As a result, nationalized day care came to be placed on the back burner. Similarly, the organization, operating from a liberal feminist perspective, tended to treat women as a homogeneous group possessing uniform concerns – in other words, those derived from a white middle and upper class perspective. By adopting this perspective it failed to recognize that women of colour and immigrant women were oppressed also as a result of the racism they experienced. In effect, the National Action Committee ignored the consequences of an entrenched racism which dictated that women of colour were less desirable citizens, resulting in the restriction of employment opportunities to the lower socio-economic rungs in which domestic labour predominated. Consequently, the women's movement came to be further divided along lines of race and class.

By the 1980s, women of colour began to shun the National Action Committee and create their own organizations.[5] At this juncture, the neoliberal discourse was gaining ground, the Keynesian Welfare State was eroding, and the National Action Committee was placed on the defensive, forced to protect the legislative and service gains that women had made over the past decade. At the same time, the organization had to confront its own race and class biases in order to retain its credibility as the voice of the women's movement. In the face of severe government cutbacks, this twofold task absorbed all of the organization's resources, leaving little to devote to the issue of nationalized day care. This process is still unfolding in the 1990s and has two consequences. First, women are still divided by race and class, thereby limiting the extent to which they can push for more inclusive legislation. Second, the crisis in the domestic sphere has intensified with the retraction of the Keynesian Welfare State, the reprivatization of many care services to the home, and the increased numbers of women forced to work. This has had the effect of ensuring that third world women will continue to be imported to perform domestic labour for middle and upper class Canadian women.

I. 1970-1990s: The Elimination of Foreign Domestic Workers' Citizenship Rights

The Department of Manpower and Immigration had full control over immigration policy regarding domestic workers by the early 1970s. The Department was divided into two branches, each of which had a different responsibility: while the Immigration branch was responsible for importing immigrants into Canada, Manpower was responsible for regulating labour–market supply.[6] Caribbean group movements had been terminated in 1968. Yet, women of colour from the third world continued to fill the demand for domestic workers in Canada, while possessing decreasing mobility rights. This process was facilitated by the Department of Manpower and Immigration, by private recruiting agencies, and the relationship of dependence between centre and periphery.

By 1971, the number of British domestic workers had declined, but the demand for them was increasing. As a result, the State instituted imigration regulations permitting non–immigrant individuals to apply for temporary work permits in 1973. This temporary worker program was implemented to discourage individuals from applying for permanent citizenship status.[7] All workers who were not granted landed status after applying through the point system were required to obtain employment visas from abroad and renew them yearly.[8] This new system deterred foreign domestic workers from seeking permanent residency.

Caribbean women, seeking to find work in domestic service in Canada, were the primary group using the system of employment visas. Using work permits as a way of entering Canada's labour market was easier and more predictable than the highly regulated point system. Caribbean women always found it difficult to secure landed status since they were forced to undergo subjective evaluations concerning the decisions they had made in their private lives, the details of their family living arrangements, and their morals. These judgments were made in accordance with prevailing racist stereotypes about black women and preconceived notions about who constituted a desirable citizen. British domestics continued to be seen as preferred citizens and, overwhelmingly, entered Canada with landed status and its attendant rights and privileges.[9] For example, 1974 witnessed 1 165 Caribbean domestics entering on employment visas compared to 131 from the United Kingdom.[10]

Foreign domestic workers could not accrue the necessary points to acquire landed status without a job offer. Canadian Immigration granted ten points for an offer which had been authorized by Canada's Manpower counselors and sent on to the person's country of origin. While the division continued to clear offers made to British subjects and citizens of other source countries, it did not clear offers made to Jamaicans, members of the main Caribbean source country. The department made this decision without providing any clear or legitimate justification for it. As a result, Jamaican women continued to be forced to enter Canada as non–immigrants.[11] By 1974, the ratio of domestic workers entering Canada as non–immigrants to those entering as immigrants was four to one.[12] A large percentage of non–immigrants were women of colour.[13]

Private placement agencies, often owned and staffed by women, played an integral role in this process. They chose jobs for domestic workers and then recommended that the women take them – all jobs were offered by the agency's own customers. These agencies, geared towards satisfying their customers (the employers), made sure that the employers would be fully satisfied by allowing them to interview the domestic before hiring took place. These Canadian women helped to entrench the prevailing system of non-immigrant domestic labour in Canada. The agencies, knowing that foreign women of colour were in a precarious economic position and desperate to work, furthered the process whereby low wages were widely accepted by foreign domestic workers. The social and economic status of domestic workers was circumscribed through this process. Lacking citizenship status, they were not afforded the privilege of mobility. They were bonded to their employers and obliged to work for low wages.[14]

By 1976, Caribbean women composed 49.7% of those entering on temporary work permits.[15] The new Immigration Act of 1976 took away women's right to apply for landed immigrant status from inside Canada once they had terminated their work contracts.[16] This Act was fully implemented in 1978.[17] Henceforth, foreign domestic workers lacking immigrant status could be forced to return to their country of origin, at their own expense, once they had finished their term of service. Alternatively, they could acquire the status of long-term non-resident.[18] The new Act thus removed domicile protections. Previously, individuals attained domicile status once they had lived in Canada for five years as permanent residents. Those possessing this status had a greater number of rights than immigrants who possessed landed status but were not domiciled.[19] With the implementation of these restrictive guidelines, the Department of Manpower and Immigration made token attempts to protect employees working on work contracts.[20]

Foreign domestic workers would only be assigned to employers who had indicated their intention to compensate their domestics fairly and provide acceptable working conditions. Fair compensation meant paychecks in accordance with the existing minimum wage of the area where the employer resided. Despite the appearance of a relationship based on reciprocal obligation, the relationship continued to be biased in favour of the employer. Domestic workers employed in private homes continued to work in an unregulated market. Employers were able to publicly promise fair remuneration but pay lower wages once the contract began.[21] Lack of regulatory mechanisms, in conjunction with domestic workers' precarious non-immigrant status, made it improbable that they would complain to immigration officials.

Moreover, domestic workers possessed few entitlement rights. Unlike Canadian women in the paid public sphere, foreign domestic workers did not have access to protective measures in the form of the social safety net. Although they had been included in the Unemployment Insurance plan at the beginning of the 1970s, this inclusion was de jure and not de facto. Domestics on employment visas could never make claims and collect unemployment insurance[22] since they were forced to leave Canada as soon as they completed their work contract.

The persistence of deeply-ingrained perceptions regarding the value of domestic labour licensed domestic workers' low status and low wages. Maternal feminism continued to provide the window through which domestic labour was viewed; that is, as women's expected donation to society. Immigration officials continued to view domestic work as culturally invisible and economically insignificant. They failed to recognize its integral importance to the nation's economy. During the 1970s, immigration policy decreased the demand value for domestic work from twelve to ten, ensuring that domestic work retained its low status and low market value.[23] Additionally, the isolation inherent in working in private homes, combined with trade unions' unwillingness to organize this employment sector – based on their perception that this work was non-work[24] – meant that these women remained in a vulnerable position.

Until the end of the 1970s, foreign domestic workers came mainly from the Caribbean. This balance began to change in 1977. At this point, although some individuals protested, the government began a systematic deportation of workers, including domestics. These deportations were directed against Caribbean domestics who had allegedly falsified their entrance documents and, interestingly, they coincided with this group's demands for greater rights and labour protections. Caribbean community organizations, viewing the deportations as a problem affecting the larger black community, organized to defend domestic workers. Between 1977 and 1979, two mass campaigns were conducted.

The first campaign, called "Save the Seven Mothers", centred on the Caribbean women who, despite their landed status, were marked for deportation. The second, the "Good Enough to Work, Good Enough to Stay" campaign, was an extension of the "Save the Seven Crusade". It concentrated on domestic work's economic and material characteristics. These two campaigns made domestic workers' living and working conditions a public issue.[25]

During this period of mobilization, the Temporary Employment Program of 1973 was described by advocacy groups and the Caribbean community as "'a revolving door of exploitation' which met the hefty demand for live-in domestic work in Canada at the lowest possible cost to both employers and the government."[26] Advocacy groups attempted to change labour laws so that they would apply to domestics. They also tried to secure landed status for domestic workers on temporary employment visas and have employers sign binding contracts.[27] These three measures were seen as critical to the improvement of domestic workers' social and economic status. All three demands were ignored. Domestics continued to be excluded de facto if not de jure from most labour laws; employers continued to have virtual control over domestics' wages and hours of work; and domestics continued to enter on temporary employment visas. Because these women lacked electoral and political rights, the only changes made as a result of these campaigns was a shift in the primary source country, from the Caribbean to the Philippines, and a greater restrictiveness in the conditions governing these women's entry into Canada.

As a result of this negative publicity, in September 1980, Lloyd Axworthy, the newly appointed Minister of Employment and Immigration, commissioned a Task Force on Immigration Practices and Procedures in order to evaluate the level of consistency between the Immigration Act of 1976 and actual immigration procedures. The Task Force was to concentrate specifically on workers with temporary work permits. The Task Force's ninety-seven page report, entitled *Domestic Workers on Employment Authorizations*, documented several areas of concern in the overall working conditions, including over-dependence on employers for both housing and money, isolation resulting from living in private homes, lack of citizenship status for some, and little or no means of taking collective action. It concluded that all these factors contributed to the exploitation of domestic workers.[28] Despite this, the Minister of Employment and Immigration ignored the measures that were recommended to help foreign domestics achieve permanent status.

In April, September, and November 1981, Lloyd Axworthy and his department officials altered the immigration regulations concerning foreign domestic workers. The practice of allowing domestic workers from the third world (primarily the Philippines) to enter Canada on temporary employment visas without landed status was to continue. British domestics, viewed as desirable citizens, were to enter with full landed status. This policy preferentially awarded points for occupational training to British domestics. Since British women, unlike Philippine and Caribbean women, often possessed formal training, they were automatically awarded ten of the fifteen maximum points.[29]

Overseas officials granted women temporary employment visas if they were deemed to possess the personal and vocational characteristics necessary to become accomplished Canadian citizens. This translated into a willingness to work as a domestic for a period of two years at a low rate of remuneration. Women granted temporary work visas were forced to remain on employment authorizations for a two-year period with assessments regarding their eligibility for landed status to occur at the end of each year. These assessments aimed to determine the applicant's potential for successful integration within Canada, and were based on the person's record of stability in household service as well as their ability to demonstrate both an improvement in their employment skills and a high level of self-sufficiency. Only women who were denied the right of landed status and were eventually to be deported were to be granted extensions for a third year.[30]

Axworthy's new program, called the Foreign Domestic Movement, invariably served the interests of employers. Theoretically, employers were required to give domestics time off to make it possible to attend up–grading courses. Employers were also supposed to contribute financially towards their workers' efforts to attend these courses. However, employers could obstruct domestics' efforts to obtain landed status since workers were forced to live in their employers' homes and work in an unregulated market. The absence of mechanisms to ensure that employers adhered to the terms of the Department of Citizenship and Immigration's employment contract meant that employers could continue to extend hours of work, pay domestics lower than the prevailing wages of the region and, by denying them time off, prevent domestics from attending the courses necessary to upgrade their skills.[31]

Most domestics were reluctant to tell immigration officials about employers who failed to keep their side of the bargain[32] since their record in household service was an important criterion in determining the level of their personal suitability for life in Canada. As one Caribbean woman who had been working as a domestic on work permits for five years stated:

> When I just started with these people I got paid minimum wage, which use to work out to $510.00 or so a month, but I don't know what happen but for the last six months I've been getting $400.00 a month. I don't ask questions, because I don't want any trouble...I don't even get my full days off...I don't say anything though, I just pretend that everything is fine...I don't want to move around too much, I don't want to create any bad feeling with the Immigration officers.[33]

Employers were required to write letters of evaluation to be used as part of the assessment. If the employer stated that the domestic was not satisfactory or complained about her performance, the letter could be used against the domestic worker.[34] Consequently, employers remained free to treat their employees as they wished, protected by "the privacy of their own homes".[35]

This freedom was in keeping with the Department of Citizenship and Immigration's traditional perception that domestic labour was, and is, not real work. Domestic workers, unlike other workers in the Canadian labour force, could not demonstrate self-sufficiency by pointing to the number of years served in their occupation. Instead, they were evaluated according to qualifications that lay outside the purview of their profession, forced to develop skills unrelated to household service work. The State categorized domestic work as being outside the area of legitimate productive labour where workers were safeguarded by collective protective measures, collective bargaining, and regulatory mechanisms.[36]

In 1985, the Canadian Federal Court outlawed the self-sufficiency clause of the pre-migration stipulations for temporary domestic workers. This resulted in a revised policy, but relatively few changes in domestics' position of dependency. Immigration officials still expected domestics to live in the homes where they were employed, although they could choose to live out with the consent of their employers. Domestics continued to be restricted to work in private homes and still had to arrive as non-immigrants on temporary work permits. They could not change jobs unless Employment and Immigration officials gave them explicit permission, although the practice of employers consenting to job changes was eliminated. Workers were expected to report any job loss so that officials could determine whether or not they were at fault. They also had to prove that they were financially responsible and they were required to report any involvement in community activities. All of these factors influenced their final evaluation.[37]

Officials still used the self-sufficiency clause in the assessment procedures, they merely took more care in the wording of their refusals. Domestics were also evaluated on the degree to which they obeyed officials' advice to upgrade their skills, their level of experience in household service, their degree of wealth, proof of skills developed in other areas, and whether or not they would be able to support their dependents. Hence, employers continued to play a crucial role in determining whether or not domestic workers would receive landed status. At the end of the 1980s, many domestics were still subjected to exploitation in the form of sexual harassment, denial of payment for overtime work, lack of choice regarding the conditions in which they lived, and lack of food.[38]

This policy, based on a racist system that designated some women, according to their colour, as less desirable citizens than others was further elaborated in the 1990s. In 1992, the Live-In Caregiver Program was instituted, thereby abolishing the Foreign Domestic Movement. This new policy ensured that domestics would still come to Canada without landed status, enjoy no occupational mobility and possess few rights. They continued to be obligated to live in the private homes where they worked and still could not change employers without the Department of Employment and Immigration's permission. As well, they had to complete the equivalent of a Canadian grade twelve educational program and obtain six months of formal training in domestic service prior to obtaining a visa.[39]

Isolation in private homes made female domestics vulnerable to abuse and sexual harassment. This continues to be the case. On average, these women work a seventy hour week at a rate of $667.42 per month after tax, food, and lodging deductions.[40] Moreover, these temporary workers continue to be forced to contribute part of their incomes to the Canada Pension and Unemployment Insurance Plans and must pay income tax. Although these deductions amount to about one month's salary, domestics on temporary permits are unable to make entitlement claims. They cannot apply for Unemployment Insurance since those who lose their jobs must immediately find a new one or leave Canada, while the Canadian Pension Plan is based on a system whereby non-citizens are expected to retire in their home country.[41]

Women who have completed all of the requirements of the Live-In Care Program and are eligible for landed status undergo an assessment that looks at all of their family members. If one family member does not pass security and medical clearance, the entire family is prevented from remaining in Canada and the domestic must return to her country of origin.[42] A second assessment is not available to these women. While other classes of immigrants may be subjected to this one-time assessment, only domestic workers on temporary work permits are required to work for several years in service before being permitted to undergo the assessment.

Since the mid-1970s, temporary work visas have been granted to anywhere between 10 000 and 16 000 foreign domestic workers a year.[43] Between 1982 and 1990 alone, the Foreign Domestic Movement program brought 67 000 domestic workers into Canada.66 Women compose ninety-eight percent of those on the program.[44] Possessing a non-immigrant status and limited civil and labour rights, they occupy a dependent position vis-à-vis their employers. The system of temporary employment visas operates to the benefit of female employers, who are supplied with a captive labour force.

II. Interests of the Canadian State

The system of temporary employment visas also served the interests of the Canadian State. By the 1970s, the Keynesian Welfare State's basic premise was beginning to break down. The idea that the State no longer had a responsibility for the collective well-being of its citizens was emerging as a cornerstone of Canadian politics. The global stratification of labour arose hand in hand with neoliberal ideas. The Canadian government began to discard its responsibilities regarding the economy. It no longer sought to regulate the domestic economy through protective legislation.[45] Within this framework, the notion of migrant workers as an international labour trend came to be approved by the Canadian government. This had a strong impact on domestic workers. Operating within the service industry, they were and continue to be needed as a flexible and mobile labour force that falls outside the jurisdiction of any trade unions.[46] Employment visas served the function of providing a captive labour force that could be disposed of at will.

This system served two of the State's interests. First, it meant that the State was not responsible for the social reproduction (education, health care, and so on) of this segment of the work-force. By avoiding the costs of raising a strong, young workforce, as well as the need to provide for them during old age, ill-health, and unemployment, the State's fiscal burden is reduced.[47] Second, third world women, denied citizenship rights, are placed in a precarious economic position where they are unable to orga-nize and demand the same rights as their Canadian counterparts, such as eliminating discrimination in the workplace and pay equity. Consequently, they are placed in a dependent position where they become a bonded labour force that performs Canadian women's domestic labour, thereby freeing the latter to improve their status by developing careers. This in turn provides the State with a standard by which it can measure its success in helping Canadian women attain gender parity.

Since women continue to be responsible for domestics work, those who are employed in the public sphere must either work an incredibly long day or hire replacement home workers. Many female employers state that they need to hire child care workers and domestics because help is not forthcoming from their male partners. Canadian employers and the State have provided little structural support for working parents.[48] The domestic worker program serves the interests of the Canadian State by decreasing the number of women demanding nationalized day care. Since some women can afford to hire replacement homeworkers at a low cost, their primary political demands lie in areas other than nationalized day care.

This inequitable system is facilitated by the center–periphery relationship. Third world countries are highly dependent on the remittances of migrant workers. As demonstrated in the previous chapter, Caribbean governments inadvertently helped to shape the restrictive guidelines that would govern domestics' working and living conditions and encouraged their citizens to take part in the domestic worker program. Up until the late 1970s, these women composed the backbone of the industry. Once Caribbean women began to mobilize for their rights, however, they came to occupy a secondary position in the program. Canada, instituting increasingly regressive policies, turned to the Philippines as the new source country.

This transition was aided by private placement agencies and the Philippine government which was seeking to find an alternate source of revenue to alleviate the country's widespread poverty. Placement agencies played the integral role of "screening" available workers to guarantee that employers will be fully satisfied.[49] These agencies played an essential role in shaping the assumption that some women – women of colour in particular – are inherently more suitable than others to perform domestic work. They relied on racial stereotypes regarding the employer's needs and the foreign women's defining characteristics when "screening" applicants.[50] As one agency operator stated, "My whole problem with the FDM [Foreign Domestic Movement] program, especially West Indian but also Filipino women, is that they are happy to be a domestic for the rest of their lives. But the FDM pressures them to upgrade. They feel pressured not to be a domestic, and then they can't do anything else but go on welfare."[51]

Once Caribbean women, emulating their white Canadian counterparts, began to mobilize for their rights, the image of the agreeable and affectionate mammy was replaced with the now dominant image of Caribbean women as "aggressive, incompetent and cunningly criminal".[52] As one agency owner asserted, "I'm at the point now, where if I hear it's an island girl on my answering machine, I won't even interview. If you're from Jamaica, I won't interview you. I know this is discrimination, but I don't have time for this... I don't want them... Jamaican girls are just dumb...".[53]

Following these events, private placement agencies began to actively recruit women from the Philippines, promoting them as thrifty, ambitious, and submissive workers.[54] Submissiveness was an especially important factor in instigating the shift from the Caribbean to the Philippines as the source country. As Arat–Koc (1989) points out, domestics are not merely hired to perform particular jobs, but for overall convenience. Obeying orders is an integral component of domestics' jobs. Thus, employers viewed "the display of deference, obedience, and submissiveness...as important, or more important than the actual [ability to do the] physical work."[55]

This shift was facilitated by the Philippine government which, since the 1970s, has actively attempted to export its women to work as domestics in other countries. The Philippines is characterized by a low level of industrialization and an underdeveloped economy. Its economy is defined by low incomes, high unemployment rates and the existence of a large reserve of workers who cannot find jobs. Seventy percent of its citizens are affected by poverty resulting in poor living conditions.[56] This economic crisis is largely the result of the Marcos dictatorship's 1979 collaboration with the International Monetary Fund–World Bank, and with the Philippine government borrowing billions of dollars to fund ineffective martial law development strategies. Soon after, the country's foreign debt balance inflated to $8.3 billion, and by 1981 the Philippines' economy was bogged down by its debt crisis. This crisis was intensified once the government adopted structural adjustment policies. By 1986, the country owed twenty-six billion dollars in external debt payments.[57]

Since the beginning of this debt crisis, various Philippine governments have used their bilateral relations as well as their multilateral organizations and activities to promote overseas employment.[58] In 1978, Marcos stated that "the export of manpower will be allowed only as a temporary measure to ease underemployment and will increasingly be restrained as productive domestic employment opportunities are created."[59] Yet this system of exporting workers, aided by Aquino and Ramos, became a permanent feature of the Philippine landscape. The country's dependence on these workers' foreign remittances meant that, by 1989, over one half of its workers were employed overseas, and had sent back over one billion dollars in remittances. Moreover, since the country is dependent on these remittances, it has been unwilling to implement mechanisms that would ensure the workers' protection, refusing, for example, to sign the Conventions and Resolutions of the International Labour Organization for the protection of migrant workers.[60] Philippine overseas contract workers[61] continue to be viewed by advanced capitalist States as a cheap labour source and continue to operate outside of the regulated market.

Currently, most of these overseas contract workers are women. Those who undertake work in areas traditionally associated with women's role, such as nursing and domestic labour, are much sought after in wealthier nations. Consequently, Filipinas have become the primary wage earners of their families by doing this kind of work for low wages in foreign countries.[62] This process is aided by private placement agencies. Placement agents, operators, and managers are usually women but, unlike the domestic workers whom they place, tend to be white and professional. Their jobs are largely about facilitating professional women's advancement in the public sphere by reducing their domestic burdens.[63]

The Canadian government has not officially recognized the social and economic changes that have taken place in the workforce, and this is reflected in its social policies. Licensed day care spaces remain limited. Although the number of licensed day care spaces in Canada increased by 600% between 1974 and 1991, 1991 witnessed 800 000 more children in unregulated day-care arrangements than were seen in 1973.[64] In 1993, the 363 000 child care spaces available could not fulfill the need. That same year, 1.4 million preschoolers (six years old and under) had mothers working in the paid public sphere.[65]

The Canadian State continues to advocate privatized methods of dealing with the increasing crisis in the domestic sphere. As of 1987, the federal child care plan consisted of a tax credit scheme. There was no mention of expanding dependable day care facilities nor of making them universally accessible. This approach has forced parents to deal with the problem on their own. Because there is no system of nationalized day care, user fees – more that $1 000 a month in some parts of Canada – account for a large percentage of day care costs.[66] The government will not give middle class families subsidies for regulated care. As a result, working parents with two or more young children can hire a live-in domestic and pay considerably less than if they place their children in a licensed care center or employ live-out caregivers.[67]

This discrepancy is possible as a result of deeply ingrained perceptions about the value of domestic labour. Domestic work, defined as housework and child care, remains women's responsibility, to be performed as "a labour of love".[68] Because it is not generally paid for and is not taken into account when calculating the gross national product, it is not perceived to be real work. It also remains physically invisible, with results that are difficult to measure. Yet this labour sustains the work force: the economy could not survive without it.[69]

The institutionalized women's movement never effectively challenged the perception that women are responsible for domestic labour. Although nationalized day care has been on the National Action Committee's agenda since the late 1970s, it did not occupy a priority position. Until the late 1980s, the organization was unwilling to support groups who advocated wages for housework. It also refused to confront the effects that society's racism had on women of colour, especially non-immigrants. Consequently, legislation governing foreign domestics' citizenship rights and working conditions continues to operate within a framework based on traditional conceptions of the value of domestic labour and women of colour.

II. The Institutionalized Women's Movement

The institutionalized women's movement unintentionally contributed to the restrictive policy regarding domestic workers. The National Action Committee, operating as a women's rights group, believed that women's equality could be achieved within the existing system. The organization adhered to liberal feminism's idea of gender equality and focused on removing barriers that restricted women's level of participation in the public sphere.[70] The National Action Committee became involved in an intimate relationship with the State once it became clear that the government wanted Canadian women's input. This relationship entrenched liberal feminism as the most prominent wing of the women's movement and established the organization as the legitimate voice of the movement.[71] The process that accomplished this, limiting Canadian women's ability to challenge the notion that domestic work is not real work, was facilitated by several factors.

First, grassroots feminists of both radical and Marxist streams adhered to the belief that women's emancipation could only occur by transforming the structure of society. As such, they were unwilling to try to effect change from within the system.[72] Second, their radical analyses of women's oppression and their hostility towards the media made them unpopular with the press.[73] While the members of the National Action Committee were familiar with the acceptable institutional channels for expressing feminist positions and were able to use an old girls' network of women in politics, business, and the media to garner support[74], grassroots feminists were both unable and unwilling to make use of these channels. As a result, by the late 1970s the media had managed to characterize the grassroots women's movement as an illegitimate group of claims seekers, and those who pushed for equal rights – that is, the National Action Committee – as the rightful representatives of women's issues.[75]

The National Action Committee viewed the State as a fairly useful instrument to effect change, one that would help establish programs to promote gender equality, increase services provided to women, and regulate on behalf of women's rights. This perception arose from the fact that until the end of the 1970s, Canadian women operated in a relatively benevolent environment. There was a great deal of similarity between the Federal Conservatives and Liberals at this time; they held similar views with respect to the desired degree of State intervention, especially in the economy. By the early 1980s, the two federal parties had adopted opposing ideological positions. The Progressive Conservative party took a right-wing stance supporting free enterprise and decentralization while the Liberals adopted a platform of greater government intervention in the economy and strong central federalism. Some neoliberal forces adhered to the position that the Keynesian Welfare State was too large and needed to be downsized by the new Conservative powers. These forces believed that minimal State intervention in private concerns was a desirable goal. Conversely, a increasing number of neoconservatives argued for the abolishment of State regulation designed to remove barriers impeding equality of opportunity.[76]

The National Action Committee initially operated as an autonomous and multi-partisan lobby group whose main purpose was to have the Royal Commission on the Status of Women's recommendations implemented.[77] Its success in establishing itself as the voice of the women's movement was the result of its ability to follow proven pressure group tactics, in other words, its willingness to compromise on points of short-term interest in order to maintain good, long-term relations with public decision-makers who had power in areas affecting women's issues.[78] This meant that the organization tended to focus on the more conservative of the Commission's recommendations, in particular, legislation that would enhance women's equality in the public sphere, such as pay equity.

While the National Action Committee claimed to represent the interests of all women during this period, the evidence suggests otherwise. The member groups listed as being part of the inaugural steering committee of April 1971 were all white middle class groups who had a specific, if somewhat narrow, perception of exactly what women's issues were.[79] While women of colour, immigrant women and working class women were involved in the organization, their concerns tended to be marginalized from the public debate surrounding women's issues. Women's organizations in the 1970s defined issues in a way that mirrored the racial and class values of their founding members.[80] They believed increasing women's representation and participation in the economy and politics was the best way to achieve their emancipation. They did not challenge the racism and classism that further limited some women's ability to compete on an equal footing in the public sphere. This conception of equality meant that the National Action Committee focused on issues such as pay equity and reproductive rights, including accessible and affordable abortion.[81]

Although these rights would help all women attain a certain level of parity, domestic workers were excluded from these gains since many of the equality–seeking measures, such as pay equity, applied only to work in the public sector. Moreover, these measures fell strictly in accordance with the individualist notion of equality of opportunity, ignoring the fact that women of colour were overwhelmingly limited to work in low paying areas in which domestic labour predominated. The lack of attention focused on the issue of child care and domestic labour meant that domestic workers would continue to be imported from third world countries, with few rights, to provide replacement home-work for the more privileged women of Canada.

At the National Action Committee's Strategy for Change Conference in 1972, a majority report with seventy–eight recommendations was made. Each suggested that the government implement new policy, but made no attempts to outline actual policy. A self–defined "radical caucus of women" composed of more than sixty women was the only group to address the issue of nationalized day care. These women demanded State–funded child care as a basic right on par with education. This was a minority view and child care was not placed on the National Action Committee's agenda of priorities.[82] Only in 1973 was any semblance of action taken. The National Action Committee recommended that the Canadian Advisory Council on the Status of Women give priority to "general and accessible child care (with the recommendation that a federal–provincial conference be held as soon as it can be thoroughly prepared)."[83]

The federal government ignored this demand as it did the more radical ones. It could do so because the National Action Committee focused on lobbying into the 1980s. By relying on this method, the National Action Committee ensured that women remained in the position of supplicants in the face of the federal government. Consensus surrounding which issues should receive priority was reached at the annual general meeting, whose purpose was to help the executive to prioritize from amongst those issues pointed out by the Royal Commission. The executive tended to be run by middle class white women in Toronto who operated within a liberal feminist framework. The National Action Committee's energies were focused on educating its members about the different methods of lobbying and not on assessing and evaluating policy, nor on creating policy proposals.[84] All of these efforts were geared toward the annual lobby that took place in Ottawa.[85] At this time, lobbying was, for the most part, a private activity.[86] Since the organization was multi-partisan, it could never use the promise of votes to sway government officials on policy issues. For these reasons, the government tended to ignore its more radical demands.

The National Action Committee, operating from within the liberal feminist perspective, did not question the well-entrenched assumption that work in the public sphere is inherently more valuable and rewarding than work in the private sphere. Consequently, although it wanted to eliminate sex-role stereotyping, it inadvertently helped to reinforce this perception. In 1979, when the group Wages for Housework applied for membership to the National Action Committee it was refused. This refusal was justified by the statement that,

> ...NAC [the National Action Committee] does not support the concept of wages for housework... What NAC is aiming for in the long run – equal opportunities, equal pay, and an end to sex role stereotyping – appears to be in contradiction to the basic goal of the Wages for Housework group: pay for housework, even the activity of keeping oneself clean and fed. The NAC executive believes this WFH goal ultimately reinforces the stereotype of woman in the home and the current division of labour by sex...NAC remains committed to the position that the only way to solve the problems of immigrant and poor women is to end sex role stereotyping and to achieve full participation in all areas of society.[87]

With this statement, the National Action Committee failed to acknowledge that some women do not consider work to be an emancipatory experience, especially if the work is underpaid and dull.[88] Moreover, it did not acknowledge the fact that because traditional conceptions regarding the low value of domestic labour remained ingrained in society's collective consciousness, many middle class women were increasing their numbers in the public sphere at the expense of non-immigrant women of colour who continued to be imported under increasingly restrictive conditions to perform this labour. The National Action Committee's refusal to support this group, in spite of Wages for Housework's arguments that the campaign could mobilize immigrant women and poor women, meant that the interests of white middle and upper class women would continue to be served in the area of domestic labour.

This policy position with regard to domestic labour and the white middle class perspective dominated the organization well into the 1980s. Thus when Caribbean domestics and the Caribbean community began to organize for their rights, the National Action Committee did not apply pressure on the government to improve their working and living conditions. Consequently, it inadvertently negated Caribbean women's claims that they had a right to citizenship and its attendant rights and privileges. In the absence of this pressure, the government was able to continue its restrictive policies with respect to foreign domestic workers during the 1980s and 1990s. These policies allowed for free-market enterprise in the area of domestic labour and were in keeping with the neoliberal discourse that was gaining ground.

At this time, the National Action Committee, aware of the inefficacy of its lobby method, was undergoing a transformation: it began to move beyond the lobby stage to create policy proposals. It subsequently initiated a process of brief-and-lobby. While the annual Ottawa lobby continued, the National Action Committee also attempted to present to parliamentary committees briefs and position papers on salient issues of policy affecting women's status.[89] These briefs and papers, however, were confined to a narrow range of subjects. Although the National Action Committee set its own agenda, it was largely responding to the agenda set by the government rather than adhering strictly to those priorities identified from within the organization. Furthermore, since the organization was working under time constraints and had limited human resources, its agenda was frequently determined by the urgency of the issues proposed by the government, as opposed to the time it would take to thoroughly study an issue.[90] The organization did not take any action geared towards improving foreign domestic workers' rights since the issue of foreign domestic workers was neither on the National Action Committee or the State's agenda.

Presenting briefs proved to be difficult. In order for the National Action Committee to arrange to be heard, it had to engage in extensive lobbying. The State did not actively try to include women's groups in the policy-making process nor did it involve them in government procedures or listen to what they had to say.[91] The National Action Committee was best able to participate in the policy-making process by relying on women active within either the Liberal or the New Democratic Party who had political influence and resources of their own.[92] These women, however, adhered primarily to a liberal feminist analysis of women's subordinate status. Consequently, they did not challenge the perception that domestic labour is not real work. This meant that foreign domestic workers were not considered to be deserving of higher wages and that a system of nationalized day care, which would alleviate the need to import foreign domestics under increasingly regressive regulations, was not viewed as essential to women's equality.

Priorities for the annual lobby were decided at the annual general meeting, while the executive committee continued to address issues as they arose during the year. The National Action Committee was forced to continue relying on members living in Toronto to serve on its executive since it had limited financial resources. The only women who could fill these positions, besides those from Toronto, were women who had the budget to travel to meetings or whose employers who would pay for their trip. These women, who tended to be both white and middle class, imported their class and race biased perspective as the dominant frame of reference. As well, the National Action Committee, viewing itself primarily as a lobby group, chose leaders who were familiar with the political system and who could comprehend the type of group that could prevail in the federal political process.[93]

All of these factors contributed to the National Action Committee ignoring the plight of foreign domestic workers and placing a system of nationalized day care at the bottom of its list of priorities, thus leaving women who could afford it to hire domestic workers. Since the State and the organization both operated according to liberal feminism's tenets, the framework of equality of opportunity prevailed as the reigning perception of gender equality. This notion implicitly accepted the division of spheres, the idea that child care was a domestic rather than a broad-based social need, and the idea that domestic work is not real work. It thus undermined the claim that women needed a system of nationalized day care in order to achieve equality.[94] Neither the State nor the National Action Committee focused on the issue as a priority. This effectively negated the possibility of women mounting a successful campaign for the right to nationalized daycare and limited foreign domestic workers' ability to demand labour rights and wages for comparable work performed in the public sphere.

The National Action Committee's lack of attention to these issues led to rifts and accusations of narrow-mindedness and exclusivity in the National Action Committee. It continued to be viewed by non-white, non-middle class, and non-central Canadian women as ineffectively representing their interests.[95] The situation was compounded by the fact that the brief-and-lobby approach is based on a complex and technical process of defining key issues. As such, it requires a certain amount of education and expertise, thereby functionally excluding women with less education and political knowledge from the pressure group process.[96] This was especially true for foreign domestic women who are often isolated in homes, lack contacts in the wider community and are unable to speak the language.

In the 1980s, immigrant women and women of colour, dissatisfied with this elitism and the failure of the institutionalized women's movement to take up issues of racism and other subjects important to them, formed their own organizations.[97] By the mid-1980s, the women's movement was still predominantly white, although it had become less middle class. Visible minority women's groups occupied a fringe position.[98] The State's method of relating to visible minority women was in part responsible for this discrepancy of representation. Although the State helped these women to establish their own groups, it tended to treat these new organizations as special interest groups, thereby indicating that these women were to be primarily defined by their immigrant and visible minority characteristics rather than by their gender. In this process, the State took credit for dealing with the issues of sexism and racism, without examining how these two issues intersected and oppressed some women more than others.[99] This was especially true for women from the third world working as domestics in Canada.

By the mid to late 1980s, many non-white and non-middle or upper class women had created their own organizations. This new wave of mobilization undermined the National Action Committee's legitimacy as the voice of Canadian women. Consequently, the organization began to address its class and race biases, attempting to move toward advocating more inclusive legislation and integrating analyses of sexism and racism into its policy platform and proposals. Yet its efforts were severely hampered by the political climate which was increasingly moving towards a neoliberal discourse. The new Conservative regime, which began in 1984 with the election of the Mulroney government, had a dire impact on the National Action Committee. First, federal funding provided to the National Action Committee, women's presses, and grassroots women's services was drastically reduced. Second, many legislators were in agreement with REAL (Real Equal and Active for Life) Women's claims and demands since the issue of reprivatization was gaining ground. This group promoted traditional female roles within the family, rejecting the pro-choice position on abortion, pay equity and equality-seeking legal rights. REAL Women also argued against State-funded child care, claiming that only a child's own mother, living at home, could provide the necessary care.[100]

Consequently, although the National Action Committee had been successful in enshrining women's right to equality in the constitution of 1982[101], by the mid-1980s it was forced to spend all its time and resources on preserving the services and gains that it had made during the previous decades. According to the Conservative government, women's groups had to engage in suitable lobbying behaviour. The government made it clear that only those women's groups who wanted, and could afford, to "jockey" for inclusion in the government's agenda and, furthermore, who would accept the curtailment of the consultative process, would be able to achieve any kind of success (albeit short-term) in terms of gaining policy objectives. The government, which felt that the National Action Committee should only involve itself with traditional women's issues, frowned upon the committee's intensified efforts to investigate the gender-related ramifications of ostensibly gender-neutral policies.[102] This limited the organization's ability to gear its activities towards more inclusive and progressive legislation and towards issues of racism that deemed some women as more desirable citizens than others.

Internally, the committee's priorities were finding new sources of funding and building a more inclusive coalition. The focus of the National Action Committee did shift from its upper middle class roots to a more middle class organization in terms of its presentation of issues.[103] Yet it was not until 1988 that the organization had changed sufficiently to appeal to women of colour.[104] Even at this stage, many women of colour and immigrant women continued to believe that there were "gatekeepers" in the National Action Committee who were preventing them from taking office and blocking their issues from inclusion in the organization's agenda. In general, these women wanted the organization to incorporate an analysis of racism into its platforms and policy proposals.[105]

By 1987, the organization's understanding of household work had deepened and MAWS (Mothers are Women) were admitted as a member group. This group wanted the National Action Committee to create child care and taxation policies that took into consideration the different effects of State-funded, universally accessible child care on one and two income families.[106] That same year, the Conservative government produced the National Strategy on Child Care. The main legislative aspect of this strategy, the Canada Child Care Act (Bill C-144), never made it past the bill stage. It died on the order paper when parliament was dissolved in 1988.[107]

By the late 1980s, most of the National Action Committee's member groups advocated the creation of State-funded child care facilities. In 1988, the organization presented its case for a system of nationalized child care before the Parliamentary Committee on Child Care. Yet the committee's report did not support this solution.[108] By the 1988 election, the State, and Canadian society in general, influenced by the anti-feminist backlash, no longer saw women's rights and issues as a priority.[109] The Mulroney government undermined its eight year old claim that it would establish a national day care program in February of 1992: the government eliminated Family Allowance payments and reduced child benefits at the same time.[110]

Although the State continues to offer subsidized day care and child tax credits, many women are unable to avail themselves of such services because of the limited number of subsidized child care spaces.[111] Additionally, child tax credits depend on the taxpayer's ability to hand in receipts proving that child care services have been payed for. Private individuals (most often elderly or immigrant women) often take care of children whose mothers cannot afford to place them in unregulated care. Approximately sixty-eight percent of mothers fall into this category. The women who provide this care, in turn, are unwilling to claim income from their work as they are often living on the poverty line. Thus, receipts and child tax credits are often not used.[112]

Right-wing ideology and discourse, based on the cornerstones of consumerism and the free market, hide the importance of these services. Moreover, use of the terms 'parent' and 'child care worker', have become central to the debate, and deflect attention away from women's pivotal concerns regarding the issue. This has had the effect of pushing the organized women's movement outside the purview of the debate and of hiding the truth about most women's daily experiences.[113] Child care continues to be women's responsibility and women in the upper income brackets (who, overwhelmingly, are white) continue to be supplied with a captive labour force from the third world. This in turn provides them with the opportunity to enhance their status by entering the paid work force without the burden of responsibility for domestic labour and child care.

Although the National Action Committee began to make nationalized day care a priority on its agenda in the late 1980s, it has only recently begun to address the issue of foreign domestic workers. Foreign domestic workers have mobilized for their rights through organizations such as INTERCEDE and the Vancouver Domestic Workers Association and have been recognized since 1986 as a legitimate interest group eligible for government funding. Yet the organized women's movement did not take up the issue of the employment and living conditions of foreign domestic workers until the 1990s.[114] The National Action Committee, a mainly white and middle class organization until the late 1980s, was uncomfortable with the issue. This was the result of two factors.

First, the fact that foreign domestics were not Canadian citizens meant that the organization did not feel the need to improve their rights. Because the National Action Committee measures gender equity in part according to how many Canadian women are working in the paid public sphere[115], the committee was not required to improve the status of domestic workers in order for it to consider that social progress was being made. Second, since many of the women who belonged to the National Action Committee were the same women who were hiring domestic workers, they were placed in a somewhat contradictory position when considering domestic workers' rights. It was only in 1990 that the organization had resolved to petition the government to give these women immigrant status and to abolish the condition that domestics live in their employers' homes if they wish to stay in Canada.[116] As women of colour and aboriginal women have begun to affect the National Action Committee's political perspective, white upper middle class feminists have started to feel challenged.[117]

The National Action Committee has begun to realize that when some women possess fewer rights than others, all women are placed at a disadvantage. Their ability to attain gender equality becomes impeded. However, many women in the organization are still resistant to giving up the privilege that is afforded them as a result of their race and class. Although Thobani, the ex-president of the National Action Committee, was a woman of colour, she resigned with the explanation that racism within the organization was impeding any true progress.

Women of colour are increasingly finding themselves with few opportunities to escape poverty and the double work day, since they are being forced to replace white women who are moving into more lucrative and prestigious positions. The poverty of dependent countries is compelling their citizens to migrate to advanced capitalist nations in order to work in race and gender-segregated occupations. This process has resulted in women of colour from the third world replacing white women in the lowest rungs of the occupational hierarchy, both in traditional pink collar jobs and in less gender divided areas of work.[118]

Internationally, women's labour is organized according to a three rung hierarchical structure. White women from developed capitalist countries are located on the top rung, while the middle rung is occupied by white women of dependent capitalist States. Women of colour, regardless of the region in which they reside, are the cheapest to employ.[119] Until white women of the middle and upper classes relinquish the privileges they derive from their race and class in the form of citizenship rights and in the area of domestic labour, the State will continue to be able to implement policies that marginalize foreign women of colour. Ultimately, this will limit Canadian women's ability to pressure the State to institute a system of nationalized day care. This is especially true in the face of the current neoliberal discourse and anti-feminist backlash that is taking place in Canada and which continues to represent a woman's decision to work in the public sphere or stay at home to perform domestic and child care duties as personal.[120]

IV. Concluding Remarks

During this period of inclusion, Canadian women were recognized as full citizen, to be included in the political and economic spheres of the nation. Yet the notion of who constituted a desirable citizen and what women's responsibilities were remained steeped in traditional stereotypes. White women continued to enter Canada as preferred citizens, while all women remained responsible for domestic work and child care. Canada continued to import women of colour from the third world to perform domestic labour in other women's homes under increasingly restrictive conditions. Lacking citizenship and mobility rights, these women were placed in a dependent position with respect to their employers. This intra-gender relationship, characterized by dominance and subordination, operated to the benefit of both female employers and the Canadian State.

Canadian women, both as individuals and through the women's movement, helped to cultivate the process by which third world women became economically, socially, and politically marginalized. Individual women, acting as private placement agents, operators, and managers, helped to exploit third world women's poverty and the conditions that created their willingness to work under sub-minimal conditions. The National Action Committee, acting as the voice of the women's movement, aided this process in indirect but equally powerful ways.

First, by adhering to a liberal feminist conception of equality, it accepted the notion that women could access the public sphere despite the traditional sexual division of labour that allocated domestic labour and child care to women. Additionally, the committee did not question the notion that domestic labour and child care were not real work. Childcare continued to be viewed as women's responsibility and as a donation that women should make to society. This in turn limited women's ability to claim the need for a system of nationalized day care in order to participate in the public sphere on an equal footing with men, since a system of nationalized day care was not viewed by the State as a legitimate demand. This meant that individual women continued to be responsible for finding individual solutions to their child care problems.

Second, the racist and classist biases of the main women's organization, the National Action Committee, meant that its perception of gender equality left the inequitable intra–gender relations that existed within Canadian society unexamined. That is, it failed to question the fact that many foreign women of colour were being imported to do Canadian women's labour in the home, thereby freeing the latter to improve their status by working in the paid work force. Nor, until the late 1980s and early 1990s, did it question the perception that white women, because of their race, were more desirable citizens and deserving of more rights. Although this situation has begun to change in the 1990s with the National Action Committee addressing racism as well as other issues surrounding foreign domestic workers, women's ability to make claims for a comprehensive system of nationalized day care remains limited. Moreover, it is doubtful that the plight of domestics will improve in the short term. A growing neoliberal discourse, a retraction of the Welfare State that is reprivatizing many caring services and thus increasing women's domestic burdens, and third world countries' dependence on migrant workers' remittances remain tangible barriers to improvements in these workers' living and working conditions.

Notes

1. Monique Bégin, "The Royal Commission on the Status of Women in Canada: Twenty Years Later," *Challenging Times: The Women's Movement in Canada and the United States* eds. Constance Backhouse and David Flaherty (Canada: McGill-Queen's University Press, 1992), 30.
2. Nancy Adamson, Linda Briskin and Margaret McPhail, *Feminists Organizing for Change: The Contemporary Women's Movement in Canada* (Toronto: Oxford University Press, 1988), 10.
3. Janine Brodie, *Politics on the Margins: Restructuring and the Canadian Women's Movement* (Nova Scotia: Fernwood Publishing Company, 1995), 13, 49–51.
4. Greta Hofmann Nemiroff and Susan McCrae van der Voet, "Feminist Research: Does it Affect Government Policy?," *Communiqu'elles* 11 (January 1985), 13–4.
5. Judy Rebick, "Unity in Diversity: The Women's Movement in Canada," *Social Policy* (Summer 1992), 48.
6. Patricia Daenzer, *Regulating Class Privilege: Immigrant Servants in Canada, 1940s-1990s* (Toronto: Canadian Scholars Press, 1993), 89.
7. Ruth Lynette Harris, *The Transformation of Canadian Policies and Programs to Recruit Foreign Labour: The Case of Caribbean Domestic Workers, 1950s-1990s* (Ph.D. Dissertation: Michigan State University, 1988), 155–6.
8. *Ibid.*, 156.
9. Patricia Daenzer, *Regulating Class Privilege: Immigrant Servants in Canada, 1940s-1990s* (Toronto: Canadian Scholars Press, 1993), 89, 91–3.
10. *Ibid.*, 103.
11. *Ibid.*, 91–2.
12. *Ibid.*, 92.
13. Ruth Lynette Harris, *The Transformation of Canadian Policies and Programs to Recruit Foreign Labour: The Case of Caribbean Domestic Workers, 1950s-1990s* (Ph.D. Dissertation: Michigan State University, 1988), 158.

14. Patricia Daenzer, *Regulating Class Privilege: Immigrant Servants in Canada, 1940s-1990s* (Toronto: Canadian Scholars Press, 1993), 89–90.

15. Ruth Lynette Harris, *The Transformation of Canadian Policies and Programs to Recruit Foreign Labour: The Case of Caribbean Domestic Workers, 1950s-1990s* (Ph.D. Dissertation: Michigan State University, 1988), 158.

16. Patricia Daenzer, *Regulating Class Privilege: Immigrant Servants in Canada, 1940s-1990s* (Toronto: Canadian Scholars Press, 1993), 97.

17. Ruth Lynette Harris, *The Transformation of Canadian Policies and Programs to Recruit Foreign Labour: The Case of Caribbean Domestic Workers, 1950s-1990s* (Ph.D. Dissertation: Michigan State University, 1988), 161.

18. Patricia Daenzer, *Regulating Class Privilege: Immigrant Servants in Canada, 1940s-1990s* (Toronto: Canadian Scholars Press, 1993), 97.

19. Ruth Lynette Harris, *The Transformation of Canadian Policies and Programs to Recruit Foreign Labour: The Case of Caribbean Domestic Workers, 1950s-1990s* (Ph.D. Dissertation: Michigan State University, 1988), 161.

20. Patricia Daenzer, *Regulating Class Privilege: Immigrant Servants in Canada, 1940s-1990s* (Toronto: Canadian Scholars Press, 1993), 97.

21. *Ibid.*, 98.

22. Makeda Silvera, *Silenced* (Toronto: Sister Vision, 1989), 10.

23. Patricia Daenzer, *Regulating Class Privilege: Immigrant Servants in Canada, 1940s-1990s* (Toronto: Canadian Scholars Press, 1993), 96.

24. Felicita O. Villasin and M. Ann Phillips, "Falling Through the Cracks: Domestic Workers and Progressive Movements," *Canadian Women Studies* 14 (1994), 88.

25. Ruth Lynette Harris, *The Transformation of Canadian Policies and Programs to Recruit Foreign Labour: The Case of Caribbean Domestic Workers, 1950s-1990s* (Ph.D. Dissertation: Michigan State University, 1988), 199, 210, 213.

26. Cited in *ibid.*, 214.

27. *Ibid.*, 223–5.

28. Patricia Daenzer, *Regulating Class Privilege: Immigrant Servants in Canada, 1940s-1990s* (Toronto: Canadian Scholars Press, 1993), 109, 111.

29. *Ibid.*, 115–6.

30. *Ibid.*, 116, 119.

31. *Ibid.*, 119, 121.

32. Makeda Silvera, *Silenced* (Toronto: Sister Vision, 1989), 9–10.

33. Savitri in *ibid.*, 45–7.

34. Patricia Daenzer, *Regulating Class Privilege: Immigrant Servants in Canada,*

1940s-1990s (Toronto: Canadian Scholars Press, 1993), 123.

35. This phrase is taken from *ibid.*, 121. And is based on Sedef Arat-Koc's title, "In the Privacy of Our Own Homes: Foreign Domestic Workers as the Solution to the Crisis in the Domestic Sphere," *Studies in Political Economy* (Spring 1989), 22–58.

36. *Ibid.*, 121.

37. *Ibid.*, 122–3.

38. *Ibid.*, 122–5. For additional information see Makeda Silvera, *Silenced* (Toronto: Sister Vision, 1989). This book is a collection of foreign domestic workers' personal narratives and provides great insights into the types of problems that they encounter.

39. Patricia Daenzer, *Regulating Class Privilege: Immigrant Servants in Canada, 1940s-1990s* (Toronto: Canadian Scholars Press, 1993), 126.

40. Michelle Smith and Marie Boti, "Exporting Lives: Stories of Filipina Migrant Workers in Canada and the Philippines," (Draft), 5.

41. Sedef Arat–Koc, "In the Privacy of Our Own Home: Foreign Domestic Workers as the Solution to the Crisis in the Domestic Sphere in Canada," *Studies in Political Economy* 28 (Spring 1989), 48–9. Between 1973 and 1979 the total revenues from Unemployment Insurance and Canada Pension Plan collected from foreign domestic workers amounted to more than eleven million dollars. *Ibid.*, 49.

42. Match International Center, *Match News* (Ottawa: Spring 1993), 3.

43. Sedef Arat–Koc, "In the Privacy of Our Own Home: Foreign Domestic Workers as the Solution to the Crisis in the Domestic Sphere in Canada," *Studies in Political Economy* 28 (Spring 1989), 36.

44. Patricia Daenzer, *Regulating Class Privilege: Immigrant Servants in Canada, 1940s-1990s* (Toronto: Canadian Scholars Press, 1993), 125. Sedef Arat–Koc, "In the Privacy of Our Own Home: Foreign Domestic Workers as the Solution to the Crisis in the Domestic Sphere in Canada," *Studies in Political Economy* 28 (Spring 1989), 34.

45. Janine Brodie, *Politics on the Margins: Restructuring and the Canadian Women's Movement* (Nova Scotia: Fernwood Publishing Company, 1995), 13–4, 16.

46. Ruth Lynette Harris, *The Transformation of Canadian Policies and Programs to Recruit Foreign Labour: The Case of Caribbean Domestic Workers, 1950s-1990s* (Ph.D. Dissertation: Michigan State University, 1988), 157.

47. Sedef Arat–Koc, "In the Privacy of Our Own Home: Foreign Domestic

Workers as the Solution to the Crisis in the Domestic Sphere in Canada," *Studies in Political Economy* 28 (Spring 1989), 47.

48. *Ibid.*, 33, 35, 43.
49. Abigail Bakan and Daiva K. Stasiulis, "Making the Match: Domestic Placement Agencies and the Racialization of Women's Household Work," *Signs: Journal of Women in Culture and Society* 20 (Winter 1995), 309.
50. *Ibid.*, 309–10.
51. Quoted in *ibid.*, 313.
52. *Ibid.*, 320.
53. Quoted in *ibid.*, 321.
54. *Ibid.*, 322–3.
55. Sedef Arat-Koc, "In the Privacy of Our Own Home: Foreign Domestic Workers as the Solution to the Crisis in the Domestic Sphere in Canada," *Studies in Political Economy* 28 (Spring 1989), 43.
56. "The Crisis of Philippine Labour Migration," *IBON Special Release*, May 1995, 7.
57. *Ibid.*, 8.
58. *Ibid.*, 9.
59. President Marcos, quoted in Henry S. Rojas, "Filipino Labour Export: An Initial Critique," (Draft: Executive Director of KAIBIGAN, 1994), 2.
60. *Ibid.*, 4.
61. These workers tend to be the most skilled of all Philippine workers, possessing years of experience under their belts and able to work for years to come. *Ibid.*, 5.
62. Michelle Smith and Marie Boti, "Exporting Lives: Stories of Filipina Migrant Workers in Canada and the Philippines," (Montreal: Center for Philippine Concerns' Women's Committee, 1995), 2.
63. Abigail Bakan and Daiva K. Stasiulis, "Making the Match: Domestic Placement Agencies and the Racialization of Women's Household Work," *Signs: Journal of Women in Culture and Society* 20 (Winter 1995), 323–4.
64. *Ibid.*, 307–8.
65. Status of Women in Canada, *Setting the Stage for the Next Century: The Federal Plan for Gender Equity* (Canada: 1995), 24.
66. Sedef Arat-Koc, "In the Privacy of Our Own Home: Foreign Domestic Workers as the Solution to the Crisis in the Domestic Sphere in

Canada," *Studies in Political Economy* 28 (Spring 1989), 35, 51. Abigail Bakan and Daiva K. Stasiulis, "Making the Match: Domestic Placement Agencies and the Racialization of Women's Household Work," *Signs: Journal of Women in Culture and Society* 20 (Winter 1995), 308.

67. Sedef Arat-Koc, "In the Privacy of Our Own Home: Foreign Domestic Workers as the Solution to the Crisis in the Domestic Sphere in Canada," *Studies in Political Economy* 28 (Spring 1989), 35.

68. *Ibid.*, 38.

69. *Ibid.*, 37-8

70. Jill Vickers, Pauline Rankin and Christine Appelle, *Politics as if Women Mattered: A Political Analysis of the National Action Committee on the Status of Women* (Toronto: University of Toronto Press, 1993), 7.

71. *Ibid*, 55.

72. *Women Unite!* (Toronto: Canadian Women's Educational Press, 1972), 9.

73. Nancy Adamson, Linda Briskin and Margaret McPhail, *Feminists Organizing for Change: The Contemporary Women's Movement in Canada* (Toronto: Oxford University Press, 1988), 62, 70.

74. Cerise Morris, "Pressuring the Canadian State for Women's Rights: The Role of the National Action Committee on the Status of Women," *Alternate Routes* 6 (1983), 90, 98.

75. Nancy Adamson, Linda Briskin and Margaret McPhail, *Feminists Organizing for Change: The Contemporary Women's Movement in Canada* (Toronto: Oxford University Press, 1988), 70.

76. Jill Vickers, Pauline Rankin and Christine Appelle, *Politics as if Women Mattered: A Political Analysis of the National Action Committee on the Status of Women* (Toronto: University of Toronto Press, 1993), 40, 59-60. For an interesting reading of how this trend has affected women and the women's movement see Janine Brodie, *Politics on the Boundaries: Restructuring and the Canadian Women's Movement* (Toronto: Robarts Center for Canadian Studies, 1995) and, by the same author, *Politics on the Margins: Restructuring and the Canadian Women's Movement* (Nova Scotia: Fernwood Publishing Company, 1994).

77. *Ibid.*, 26.

78. Cerise Morris, "Pressuring the Canadian State for Women's Rights: The Role of the National Action Committee on the Status of Women," *Alternate Routes* 6 (1983), 91.

79. The Canadian Federation of Business and Professional Women, the Canadian Federation of University Women, the Canadian Home Economics Association, the Canadian Union of Public Employees, the Catholic Women's League of Canada, the Federated Women's Institute of Canada, the Federation of Labour (Ontario), the Federation of Women Teachers Association of Ontario, the National Chapter of Canada, the Imperial Order of the Daughters of the Empire, the National Council of Jewish Women of Canada, the National Council of Women in Canada, the New Feminists, the Women's Coalition, the Women's Liberation Movement (Toronto), and the YWCA were the groups which formed part of the National Action Committee's inaugural steering committee. Nancy Adamson, Linda Briskin and Margaret McPhail, *Feminists Organizing for Change: The Contemporary Women's Movement in Canada* (Toronto: Oxford University Press, 1988), 52.

80. *Ibid.*, 60.

81. For an in-depth reading of the National Action Committee's evolution vis-à-vis its goals and membership spanning the 1970s through the 1990s see Jill Vickers, Pauline Rankin and Christine Appelle, *Politics as if Women Mattered: A Political Analysis of the National Action Committee on the Status of Women* (Toronto: University of Toronto Press, 1993).

82. Jill Vickers, Pauline Rankin and Christine Appelle, *Politics as if Women Mattered: A Political Analysis of the National Action Committee on the Status of Women* (Toronto: University of Toronto Press, 1993), 74–6.

83. Quoted in *ibid.*, 80.

84. *Ibid.*, 74, 76, 99.

85. Cerise Morris, "Pressuring the Canadian State for Women's Rights: The Role of the National Action Committee on the Status of Women," *Alternate Routes* 6 (1983), 97.

86. Jill Vickers, Pauline Rankin and Christine Appelle, *Politics as if Women Mattered: A Political Analysis of the National Action Committee on the Status of Women* (Toronto: University of Toronto Press, 1993), 52.

87. Kay Macpherson, "Politics Within the Women's Movement," *Status of Women News* 5 (Summer 1979), 6.

88. Jill Vickers, Pauline Rankin and Christine Appelle, *Politics as if Women Mattered: A Political Analysis of the National Action Committee on the Status of*

Women (Toronto: University of Toronto Press, 1993), 107.

89. Cerise Morris, "Pressuring the Canadian State for Women's Rights: The Role of the National Action Committee on the Status of Women," *Alternate Routes* 6 (1983), 97.

90. Greta Hofmann Nemiroff and Susan McCrae van der Voet, "Feminist Research: Does it Affect Government Policy?," *Communiqu'elles* 11 (January 1985), 13–4.

91. *Ibid.*, 15–6.

92. Cerise Morris, "Pressuring the Canadian State for Women's Rights: The Role of the National Action Committee on the Status of Women," *Alternate Routes* 6 (1983), 98.

93. Jill Vickers, Pauline Rankin and Christine Appelle, *Politics as if Women Mattered: A Political Analysis of the National Action Committee on the Status of Women* (Toronto: University of Toronto Press, 1993), 76.

94. See Nancy Fraser, "Talking About Needs: Interpretive Contests as Political Conflicts in Welfare–State Societies," *Ethics* 99 (January 1989), 291–313. This article discusses the ways in which entitlement claims are legitimated by the state and how women are often coopted in the process of partially meeting their demands. It is particularly insightful in the context of the debate surrounding child care.

95. Cerise Morris, "Pressuring the Canadian State for Women's Rights: The Role of the National Action Committee on the Status of Women," *Alternate Routes* 6 (1983), 95. For a perception of this process, see Maxine McKensie, "You Mean I Still Ain't?," *Breaking the Silence* 5 (1987), 8–9.

96. Cerise Morris, "Pressuring the Canadian State for Women's Rights: The Role of the National Action Committee on the Status of Women," *Alternate Routes* 6 (1983), 103.

97. Judy Rebick, "Unity in Diversity: The Women's Movement in Canada," *Social Policy* (Summer 1992), 48.

98. Sandra Burt, "The Women's Movement: Working to Transform Public Life," *The Women's Movement: Working to Transform Public Life*, eds. James P. Bickerton and Alain G. Gagnon (Ontario: Broadview Press, 1994), 220.

99. Linda Carty and Dionne Brand, "'Visible Minority' Women – A Creation of the Canadian State," *Resources for Feminist Research* 17 (188), 41.

100. Sylvia Bashevkin, "Building a Political Voice: Women's Participation and Policy Influence in Canada," *Women and Politics Worldwide*, eds. Barbara J. Nelson and Najma Chowdhury (USA: Yale University Press, 1994), 149, 155.

101. This right is enshrined in sections 15 and 28 of the constitution. These read as follows:

> Section 15 (1) Every individual is equal before and under the law and has the right to equal protection and equal benefit of the law without discrimination and, in particular, without discrimination based on race, nation or ethnic origin, colour, religion, sex, age, or mental or physical disability.
>
> 15 (2) Subsection (1) does not preclude any law, program or activity that has as its object the ameliorative condition of the disadvantaged individuals or groups including those that are disadvantaged because of race, national or ethnic origin, colour, religion, sex, age or mental or physical disability...
>
> 28 Notwithstanding anything in this charter, the rights and freedoms referred to in it are guaranteed equally to male and female persons.

102. Jill Vickers, Pauline Rankin and Christine Appelle, *Politics as if Women Mattered: A Political Analysis of the National Action Committee on the Status of Women* (Toronto: University of Toronto Press, 1993), 222-3.

103. Beverly in Amy Gottlieb, ed., "What About Us? Organizing Inclusively in the National Action Committee on the Status of Women – A Roundtable Discussion Facilitated By Maureen Fitzgerald and Amy de Wolff," *And Still We Rise: Feminist Political Mobilizing in Contemporary Canada*, ed. Linda Carty (Toronto: The Women's Press, 1992), 372-3.

104. Judy in *ibid.*, 374.

105. Jill Vickers, Pauline Rankin and Christine Appelle, *Politics as if Women Mattered: A Political Analysis of the National Action Committee on the Status of Women* (Toronto: University of Toronto Press, 1993), 166-7.

106. *Ibid.*, 252, 258.

107. Sylvia Bashevkin, "Building a Political Voice: Women's Participation and Policy Influence in Canada," *Women and Politics Worldwide*, eds.

Barbara J. Nelson and Najma Chowdhury (USA: Yale University Press, 1994), 153–4.

108. Jill Vickers, Pauline Rankin and Christine Appelle, *Politics as if Women Mattered: A Political Analysis of the National Action Committee on the Status of Women* (Toronto: University of Toronto Press, 1993), 237, 262.

109. Judy Rebick, "Unity in Diversity: The Women's Movement in Canada," *Social Policy* (Summer 1992), 54.

110. Ruth Roach Pierson, "The Politics of the Domestic Sphere," *Canadian Women's Issues: Volume II*, eds. Ruth Roach Pierson and Marjorie Griffin Cohen (Toronto: James Lorimer & Company, 1995), 17.

111. *Ibid.*, 17, 22.

112. *Ibid.*, 17. Lois Harder, "The Trouble with Democracy: Child Care in Ontario and the Politics of Representation," *And Still We Rise: Feminist Political Mobilizing in Contemporary Canada*, ed. Linda Carty (Toronto: The Women's Press, 1993), 245.

113. Lois Harder, "The Trouble with Democracy: Child Care in Ontario and the Politics of Representation," *And Still We Rise: Feminist Political Mobilizing in Contemporary Canada*, ed. Linda Carty (Toronto: The Women's Press, 1993), 251–2, 254.

114. Felicita O. Villasin and M. Ann Philips, "Falling Through the Cracks: Domestic Workers and Progressive Movements," *Canadian Woman Studies* 14 (1994), 88–9.

115. Patricia Daenzer, *Regulating Class Privilege: Immigrant Servants in Canada, 1940s-1990s* (Toronto: Canadian Scholars Press, 1993), 9.

116. Felicita O. Villasin and M. Ann Philips, "Falling Through the Cracks: Domestic Workers and Progressive Movements," *Canadian Woman Studies* 14 (1994), 88–9.

117. Judy in Amy Gottlieb, ed., "What About Us? Organizing Inclusively in the National Action Committee on the Status of Women – A Roundtable Discussion Facilitated by Maureen Fitzgerald and Amy de Wolff," *And Still We Rise: Feminist Political Mobilizing in Contemporary Canada*, ed. Linda Carty (Toronto: The Women's Press, 1992), 380.

118. Linda Carty, "Combining Our Efforts: Making Feminism Relevant to the Changing Sociality," *And Still We Rise: Feminist Political Mobilizing in Contemporary Canada*, ed. Linda Carty (Toronto: The Women's Press, 1992), 15.

119. *Ibid.*, 14.

120. Ruth Roach Pierson, "The Politics of the Domestic Sphere," *Canadian Women's Issues: Volume II* eds. Ruth Roach Pierson and Marjorie Griffin Cohen (Toronto: James Lorimer & Company, 1995), 15.

Conclusion

This book has stressed that an enduring feature of modern Canadian society is the subordinate position of women. This position arises from the fact that women remain responsible for domestic labour and child care. Yet, their gender oppression is overlaid by internal divisions along lines of race and class. For some middle and upper class Canadian women, this burden can be alleviated by hiring a replacement homeworker. For other women, particularly women of colour and working class women, this private solution is unavailable. Consequently, they are overwhelmingly forced to work a double day. For many immigrant women of colour, their double day increasingly takes place in the home as they are forced to work in other women's homes, performing domestic duties for low wages.

Today, this position is reinforced by the global division of labour. The Canadian State continues to import foreign domestic labourers to work for low wages under adverse conditions, with no labour and mobility rights. Women of colour from the third world tend to occupy the lowest socioeconomic rung in the globalized market. Living in poor countries, they are often compelled to perform labour that pays little. Canada is seen by these women as an economic opportunity. Even if they are forced to work as domestics, the wages are higher than any they might receive in their country of origin, and the promise of citizenship status and citizenship rights offers the possibility of entering more lucrative areas of employment. Consequently, these women are often willing to work as domestics for a period of indentureship.

The Canadian State and third world source nations have taken advantage of these women's desperation, the former in order to find a cheap supply of domestics for its own citizens while limiting social expenditures, the latter by encouraging their female citizens to take part in the domestic worker program in order to capitalize on the workers' remittances. The end result has been a mistress–servant relationship that is characterized by domination and subordination. This intra–gender relationship is mediated by a complex matrix of race and class that parallels that of the center–periphery relationship. In the global system of stratification of labour, white Canadian women tend to be found in the higher socio–economic brackets while foreign women of colour are forced into a dependent position regarding the former. Ultimately, white middle and upper class Canadian women have certain privileges, many of which are derived from their citizenship status and are unavailable to women of colour. These privileges, however, rely on the ability to exploit foreign women of colour. For it is only by hiring these women to work as domestics that Canadian women are freed from their domestic duties and are able to gain access to the public sphere in order to improve their own status.

The State has an interest in maintaining restrictive immigration policies concerning foreign domestics since they limit the demands that women place on the State. Because some Canadian women benefit from this policy, the institutionalized women's movement has been slow to realize that these policies have ultimately weakened their bargaining power with the State. Women's divisions along lines of race and class have allowed the State to create policies that pit different groups of women against each other, which in turn has limited the possibility of effective coalitions among them. By the time recognition of this process took root, the mistress–servant relationship was well-entrenched in Canadian society. This has meant that domestic workers, especially foreign domestic workers, find themselves at the bottom of the heap, as witnessed by their situation over the last hundred years which, despite twists and turns, has not improved much.

In fact, the Canadian State's immigration policies concerning foreign domestic workers have become increasingly regressive over the course of the past century. This shift has coincided with changes in the race of the women in the domestic worker program. Up until 1947, domestics were recruited from Britain. Viewed as desirable citizens, they were granted full citizenship and labour mobility rights. Although domestics were admitted from areas other than the traditional source country in the post-war period, it was only in 1955 that Caribbean women were admitted to the program and different standards were applied. While British domestics continued to enter Canada with full citizenship and citizenship rights, Caribbean women's citizenship and labour rights were curtailed. By the 1960s and 1970s, the country of origin and the race of domestic servants had changed from predominantly British and white to women of colour from the third world. As these women came to compose the backbone of the industry, they were subject to increasingly restrictive guidelines governing their working and living conditions. They continue to have few labour, political, or civil rights. As such, they are largely unable to demand the same rights that are granted to other women living in Canada. Ultimately, they have become marginalized and are forced to work in virtual captivity for low wages and under adverse conditions.

Although State policies have allowed Canadian women to increase their participation in the public sphere, the public–private divide and its attendant value structure remains much the same as it appeared at the turn of the century: domestic labour and child care remain women's responsibility and are valued less than work performed in the public sphere. This is largely the result of immigration policies that have facilitated the perpetuation of the mistress–servant relationship. Historically, this relationship has underpinned the organized women's movement's failure to question the public–private divide's value structure. At no point in time did the organized women's movement formally advocate policies of transformation.

According to Trimble (1990), the aim of transformative policies is to alter radically the essential values of society so that work in the private domain is no longer considered less worthy than that performed in the public domain. These policies are also directed towards preventing the gendering of roles and their respective domains. The aim is for domestic labour and child care to be recognized and valued for their contribution to the economy and to be viewed as equal in importance to work performed in the public sphere. During the first and second waves of the women's movement, women who did advocate these policies were marginalized from the political debate surrounding Canadian women's rights.

Changes in domestic workers' rights have not only been a result of State policies but also the result of the women's movement's influence at both a material and ideological level. The women's movement and individual women have sometimes actively lobbied for immigration policies that discriminate against non-white domestic workers. In other cases, the movement's demands for emancipation have been achieved on the backs of domestic workers, thereby reflecting the internal contradictions of the women's movement. These inner contradictions have been most explicit in the dominance of maternal and liberal feminism within the movement itself.

During the late nineteenth and early twentieth centuries, women reformers actively helped to shape the terms under which domestics immigrated to Canada. British women "of the right sort" were recruited by women's organizations in both Britain and Canada to take part in Canada's nation-building enterprise. British women were not merely recruited to work as domestics, but were destined to become future mothers of the nation and guardians of the race. Seen as desirable and deserving citizens, these women were to be granted the same rights as Canadian women.

Under this immigration system, black women were unable to enter Canada as citizens. Although a special group movement of women from Guadeloupe was admitted to Canada in 1910-11, this practice was quickly terminated. Black women were viewed as unassimilable and thus a threat to the reformers' vision of an organic society based on Anglo-Saxon middle class morality and the traditional family structure. As such, these women were desired neither as citizens nor as mothers. It was at this point that Canada's "racialized"[1] immigration policy with respect to domestic workers began.

Reform women's influence was not confined to direct intervention in immigration regulations. Their reform activities also had an impact on domestic workers by influencing the broader societal context in which responsibility for and value of domestic labour and child care were determined. All of these women's reform activities were geared towards strengthening the family and women's role within it. Reformers, explicitly accepting that women were responsible for domestic work and child care, highlighted women's altruistic, caring and devoted nature. As a result, although women's reform activities had the effect of expanding the range of socially acceptable occupations for women, women were confined to jobs that were extensions of their traditional maternal role. For black Canadian women, race created an additional restriction on their employment opportunities, confining them to domestic service.

Reform women neither questioned the sexual division of labour nor the idea that some women, because of their race, should be restricted to certain types of employment. Reformers effectively accepted the racist notion that black women were inferior, and implicitly embraced the public–private divide. Once they came to dominate the suffrage movement, their maternal feminist arguments ensured that white middle and upper class women would have more rights than non-white working class women, despite the fact that all Canadian women were granted the same formal legal rights.

This was largely the result of the way in which domestic labour and child care were framed. Women's reform activities and their maternal feminist arguments ensured that women would continue to be responsible for domestic labour. Since women's maternal function and their moral force were highlighted in the demand for suffrage, child care could not be presented as a broad social need. Instead, it was framed as children's need for full-time care by a stay-at-home mother and thus considered a domestic need.[2]

This was possible due to the fact that transformative policies were never advocated during the first wave of the women's movement. These policies could not be advocated for two reasons. First, equal rights feminists, with their radical conception of gender equality, were the only members of the suffrage movement that had the possibility of advancing this type of demand. Yet they were shunted out of the suffrage movement. With their exclusion, the organized women's movement lost all hope of attaining a unified womanhood and a radical reordering of society. Second, maternal feminists' arguments, enforcing the notion that the home was women's domain, effectively ruled out the possibility of divorcing the public–private divide from gender.

Moreover, although middle and upper class white women of the first wave of the women's movement accepted the idea that all women should be granted the same formal–legal rights in the form of the vote and legal personhood, they implicitly accepted the notion that they were better able than other women to exercise their rights in the public sphere. Ignoring black and working class women's concerns had the effect of relegating these women to the lower socio–economic brackets and of marginalizing them from the public debate surrounding women's issues and rights. Thus, society's conception of gender equality remained rooted in the reality of middle and upper class white women who could afford to hire replacement homeworkers.

Additionally, since the public–private divide and its attendant value structure were not questioned by these women, the idea that private sphere duties were not as valuable to the economy as those that take place in the public sphere remained within Canada's collective frame of reference. Consequently, the notion that child care and domestic labour are not real work and are thus undeserving of a high level of remuneration was not challenged. Domestic labour and child care continued to be viewed by the Canadian State as the donation that women should make to society. This effectively meant that once Canadian women were granted the right to vote and the status of legal personhood, only white middle and upper class women who could afford to hire replacement homeworkers were fully able to enjoy their formal legal rights of citizenship.

The system governing the immigration of domestic workers remained largely unchanged until the end of the Second World War. After World War Two, changes in immigration policy took place, the most notable of which was the admittance of non-British women into Canada as domestic servants. Canadian women, increasingly entering the public sphere, were in need of a new supply of domestic workers since British women and black Canadian women were no longer willing to do this work. These Canadian women began pressuring immigration officials to provide them with a new source of domestic workers who would be willing to work for low wages. Although black women from the Caribbean were admitted in 1955 to work as domestics, they were not granted the right to collective measures of protection, such as Unemployment Insurance, that was available to both their British couterparts and other workers in the Canadian workforce. Although they were granted landed status upon arrival, the threat of deportation and termination of the scheme should this group of women not complete their terms of service meant that they enjoyed no mobility rights.

The predominantly middle and upper class white female employers had a hand in influencing the immigration policy that meted out different treatment to Caribbean domestics. In the 1950s, these women specifically requested that Caribbean women be admitted to Canada as domestics, citing them as an inexpensive and plentiful source. Female employers actively encouraged immigration officials to take advantage of the Caribbean nations' legacy of poverty in order to improve their own status. They intervened in the 1950s and 1960s deliberations concerning whether or not to include domestic workers under the Unemployment Insurance plan. Aware that Unemployment Insurance would afford domestics some measure of protection against abuse, they expressed concerns about including them in the plan. Knowing that these women were poor and desperate to work in Canada, Canadian women were unwilling to grant them the same labour protections that they themselves enjoyed.

An awareness of class interests and preconceived ideas of who was deserving of citizenship rights permeated these employers' actions. They helped to expand Canada's racialized immigration policy. British domestics largely continued to enter Canada with full citizenship and citizenship rights, while Caribbean domestics were subjected to restrictive terms of employment with no citizenship rights. The ostensibly universal point system that was instituted in 1968 ultimately had the effect of further limiting Caribbean domestics' ability to acquire citizenship and citizenship rights, since only British domestics tended to be able to amass enough points to enter Canada. This process was completed with the implementation of the Temporary Employment Authorization Program in 1973 which was geared towards providing Canadian women with domestics willing to work for low wages and restricting citizenship to members of preferred nations.

This two-tiered immigration policy was facilitated by both the second wave of the women's movement and individual women acting as private placement agency owners, operators, and managers. Like its first wave predecessor, the second wave of the organized women's movement failed to question the notion that domestic labour is not real work. Even the National Action Committee, acting as the voice of Canadian women and operating within the liberal framework of equality of opportunity, did not raise this challenge until the late 1980s. By advocating an increase in women's participation in the public sphere as the route to gender equality, the organization effectively legitimized the idea that work in the public sphere is inherently more valuable than that performed in the private sphere. In this way, it reinforced the "physical, economic and ideological invisibility of domestic labour"[3] and child care. Consequently, immigration regulations governing domestics' working and living conditions reflected the well-entrenched perception that domestic workers are not essential to the proper functioning of the economy.

Transformative policies could not be advanced during this period due to the divisions between grassroots and institutionalized groups and their very different perceptions of how to achieve gender equality. Since the National Action Committee acted as the representative of Canadian women and because it adhered to a liberal feminist analysis, the organization's influence on the State was greater than that of grassroots groups. Its goals were in keeping with the predominant conception of equality of opportunity. As such, it did not question the hierarchical value structure associated with the public–private divide. This limited its ability to press the State for legislation geared towards transforming the structure of Canadian society.

Furthermore, middle and upper class white women once again came to dominate the movement during the second wave. Their perceptions and viewpoints helped to inform policies the State made with respect to Canadian women. Since the State looks to the National Action Committee for input in the policy-making process where women are concerned, the organization's liberal feminist stance informs and legitimates most of the policies that it makes. Simultaneously, however, the State looks to the organizations of women of colour when it wants to deal with issues of racism. The State thus manages to limit these women's demands to issues of racism by emphasizing their race and their immigrant status as their attributes that are most deserving of public attention. The State constitutes foreign domestic workers as a special interest group deserving of State funding, but for which it is not ultimately responsible. Because these women are foreigners they are not thought to deserve the same rights as the rest of women in Canada. In this way, the State is able to address issues of racism and sexism without having to examine their interconnectedness and implement policies that would address some of these inequities.

Although the National Action Committee began to accept as members groups that supported the position advanced by Wages for Housework groups in 1987, its failure to challenge the traditional view of domestic labour in the earlier era meant that this support had a limited effect. The organization's earlier legitimation had contributed to the reinforcement of society's view of domestic labour. Moreover, women's rights were being subjected to a backlash during the late 1980s. This backlash has continued throughout the 1990s, limiting the National Action Committee's ability to influence immigration policy in a positive manner.

Additionally, the organization's failure to address issues of racism has adversely affected foreign domestic workers' status. By advancing the position that increasing women's representation in the public sphere would allow women to attain gender parity, the National Action Committee aided the State in implementing policies that treat women as a homogenous group and thus ignore differences that arise as a result of race and class. Non-white women are generally found in the lower socioeconomic brackets. Once foreign domestic workers acquire citizenship status they are often limited by society's racism to work in areas related to housework or child care that pays low wages. The organization's failure to address the fact that racism confined these women to low paid jobs in the areas of domestic labour and child care was most notable in the period between 1977 and 1979 when Caribbean domestics mobilized to increase their rights. The National Action Committee did not lend its support to these women and thus unwittingly legitimated the restrictive policies that limited their citizenship and citizenship rights.

Although the organization is currently grappling with the plight of foreign domestic workers, its own problems with racism and society's deeply ingrained perceptions about the value of domestic labour have limited the extent of its support. White middle and upper class women in the National Action Committee's member organizations have an interest in main-taining regressive immigration policies regarding domestic servants as they are able to improve their status by hiring replacement home workers. Paying domestics low wages, they gain tangibly by being able to pursue high paying careers in the public sphere. Were domestics' rights increased, these Canadian women would be forced to pay higher wages for both child care and domestic workers. This can be attributed to the fact that domestic labour and child care continue to be seen as women's responsibility, thereby limiting the alternate possibility of a system of nationalized day care that would alleviate women's domestic burdens.

Private placement agents, owners, operators, and managers have also helped to shape these regressive policies. Since the 1970s, white middle and upper class Canadian women have helped to recruit third world women of colour to work as domestics in private homes. They have capitalized on third world women's poverty as well as their desperation to enter Canada and attain citizenship and its attendant rights. As Caribbean women began to mobilize for their rights in the late 1970s, these Canadian women acted as "gatekeepers"[4] by limiting Caribbean women's ability to access the domestic worker program. By providing employers and the Canadian State with an alternate source of domestic labourers, Caribbean women were placed in a marginal position whereby they were unable to demand the same rights that had been granted to Canadian women; that is, formal legal rights that are widely equated with human rights.

Additionally, by providing Philippine women with an example of the negative effects of mobilizing, these professional women ensured that Philippine women would continue to work in Canada as domestics for low wages and under adverse conditions. Ultimately, Canadian women's activities have made sure that the State does not have to reconsider its traditional perception of domestic work as not being real work, since some of the State's own citizens are freed by foreign domestic workers to work in the public sphere. Consequently, Canada's form of social organization that privileges whites over non-whites and the middle and upper classes over the working class has not been altered. This has meant that State policies concerning Canadian women treat all women as a homogeneous group, ignoring differences that arise from their race and class. This has reinforced divisions among women and these divisions in turn have negatively affected the strength of the organized women's movement.

Women of different races and classes often find that their interests are at odds with one another and thus, in many instances, are unable to act as a unified group with a set of common interests. Women of colour continue to perceive the National Action Committee as representing white middle and upper class women's concerns. Since women of colour tend to fall overwhelmingly into the lowest socioeconomic brackets and often work in areas associated with domestic labour, many perceive the National Action Committee's position of equality of opportunity as racially and class biased. This is partially the result of the organization's failure to fully address the issues of domestic labour's proper economic worth and the predicament of foreign domestics. While the National Action Committee has attempted to incorporate an analysis of racism into its platforms and policy proposals in recent years, class and race divisions among Canadian women persist. This is largely the result of white committee members who continue to resist the idea that they might have to give up some of their privileges during the short-term in order for true gender equality to evolve.[5]

Immigration policy concerning domestic workers, while having the effect of partially meeting the demand for child care and domestic labour, has also had the effect of reinforcing pre-existing divisions among women based on race and class. The National Action Committee's failure to challenge the idea that domestic labour is not real work and that women of colour are not as deserving of citizenship and citizenship rights has meant that the State is able to accommodate some women's need for domestic labourers at the expense of other women. Although historically it has largely been white middle and upper class women who have been able to benefit from these policies, the negative consequences of these policies have affected all Canadian women. All women ultimately remain responsible for domestic labour and child care and those who cannot afford to hire replacement homeworkers are forced to work a double day. Moreover, the mistress-servant relationship places some women in the position of oppressing others. Although this relationship serves the function of meeting the needs of some privileged Canadian women, it has had the effect of placing all Canadian women at a disadvantage in that they are unable to demand a system of nationalized child care. Divisions among women based on race and class limit Canadian women's ability to act as a unified group in the demand for a system of nationalized day care. Moreover, the framework within which domestic labour is currently viewed has meant that a system of nationalized day care in keeping with transformative policies is not currently politically feasible.

Since the mid–1980s, the institutionalized women's movement has been operating on the defensive, attempting to protect the gains in services that it achieved over the course of the 1970s and early 1980s. This has had especially deleterious effects in the case of child care. The State's unwillingness to support a system of nationalized child care and its adherence to the method of individual responsibility for child care are in keeping with well-entrenched perceptions about the sexual division of labour. They are also in keeping with the rise of neoliberal governing practices. Overall, this policy has meant that women's domestic burdens have increased. Yet, this policy affects women differently, depending on their race and class.

Although some subsidized day care spaces exist, these are not based on the belief that child care is a societal responsibility, nor do they recognize that this work makes an economic contribution to the national economy. The National Action Committee's demand for gender equality based on equality of opportunity meant that State policies would only be directed towards providing external support for women's home care duties and not towards improving the status of domestic duties or towards changing societal attitudes about women's responsibility for them. These inclusionary policies are seen by the State as facilitating women's participation in the public sphere, but since many of the services created through these policies are not seen as unalterable features of the Canadian landscape they may be retracted at will.

The practice of retracting services has become an increasingly popular trend since the late 1980s. This is especially true where caring services are concerned. The neoliberal discourse and feminist backlash that emerged in the late 1980s have increasingly delegitimized women's demands for greater equality-enhancing services. Policy-makers are not only unwilling to improve the system of subsidized day care but they are in the process of retracting this system. In effect, the State no longer sanctions expenditures in this domain. This has ultimately had the effect of decreasing the women's movement's bargaining power with the State and of reinforcing some women's dependence on restrictive immigration policies concerning domestic workers.

The State has played a crucial role throughout the process of creating this intra–gender hierarchy in the realm of domestic labour. Although it has improved the status of Canadian women over the course of the past century, it has improved some women's status more than others. State policies have ensured that some white middle and upper class women gain a number of privileges that are not available to working class women or women of colour. Moreover, these same middle and upper class white women have gained many privileges at the expense of women of colour. Despite the fact that all women are treated equally under the law, the manner in which the State has approached the issue of domestic labour has meant that Canadian women are profoundly unequal. Moreover, State policies concerning foreign women of colour have emphasized and deepened this inequality. Consequently, the State, while appearing to be neutral and addressing the issue of gender oppression, has been able to implement policies that affect women differently depending on their social location. This in turn is jointly determined by their race and class.[6]

When this historical process is considered from the viewpoint of those at the bottom, especially female foreign domestic workers, one can see how it has contributed to their plight and to the internal stratification of Canadian women. It also becomes apparent how this process has reinforced divisions within the organized women's movement, which in turn have affected its capacity for militant and effective action. Such a picture, in all its complexity, is derived from the socialist–feminist analysis that informed this essay and highlighted the way the different factors of race and class affect the women's movement and its involvement with the State.

Notes

1. Vic Satzewich, "Racism and Canadian Immigration Policy: The Government's View of Caribbean Migration, 1962–1966," *Canadian Ethnic Studies* 21 (1989), 79.
2. Nancy Fraser, "Talking About Needs: Interpretive Contests as Political Conflicts in Welfare-State Societies," *Ethics* 99 (January 1989), 300.
3. Sedef Arat-Koc, "In the Privacy of Our Own Home: Foreign Domestic Workers as the Solution to the Crisis in the Domestic Sphere in Canada," *Studies in Political Economy* 28, (Spring 1989), 37.
4. Abigail Bakan and Daiva Stasiulis, "Making the Match: Domestic Placement Agencies and the Racialization of Women's Household Work," *Signs: Journal of Women in Culture and Society* 20 (Winter 1995), 304.
5. Felicita O. Villasin and M. Ann Philips, "Falling Through the Cracks: Domestic Workers and Progressive Movements," *Canadian Woman Studies* 14 (1994), 89.
6. Melanie Randall, "Feminism and the State: Questions for Theory and Practice," *Resources for Feminist Research* 17 (1988), 14.

Bibliography

Feminist Theory

Adams, Mary Louise. "There's No Place Like Home: On the Place of Identity in Feminist Politics." *Feminist Review* 31 (1989): 22–33.

Agnew, Vijay. "Canadian Feminism and Women of Color." *Women's Studies International Forum* 16.3 (1993): 217–227.

Albrecht, Lisa and Rose M. Brewer. "Bridges of Power: Women's Multicultural Alliance for Social Change." In *Bridges of Power: Women's Multicultural Alliances.* Eds. Lisa Albrecht and Rose M. Brewer. USA: New Society Publishers, 1990. 1–22.

Alperin, Davida J. "Social Diversity and the Necessity of Alliances: A Developing Feminist Perspective." In *Bridges of Power: Women's Multicultural Alliances.* Eds. Lisa Albrecht and Rose M. Brewer. USA: New Society Publishers, 1990. 23–33.

Andrew, Caroline. "Women and the Welfare State." *Canadian Journal of Political Science* 17.4 (1984): 667–683.

Barret, Michele and Mary McIntosh. "Ethnocentrism and Socialist-Feminist Theory." *Feminist Review* 20 (1985): 23–47.

de Beauvoir, Simone. *The Second Sex.* Trans. H. M. Parshley. New York: Bantam Books, 1969.

Brewer, Rose M. "Theorizing Race, Class and Gender: The New Scholarship of Black Feminist Intellectuals and Black Women's Labour." In *Theorizing Black Feminism: The Visionary Pragmatism of*

Black Women. Eds. Stanlie M. James and Abena P. A. Busia. London: Routeledge, 1993.

Briskin, Linda. "Identity Politics and the Hierarchy of Oppression." *Feminist Review* 35 (1990): 102–106.

Bunch, Charlotte. "Making Common Cause: Diversity and Coalitions." In *Bridges of Power: Women's Multicultural Alliances.* Eds. Lisa Albrecht and Rose M. Brewer. USA: New Society Publishers, 1990. 42–67.

Cohen, Yolande. (1982). "Thoughts in Women and Power." In *Feminism in Canada: From Pressure to Politics.* Eds. Angela Miles and Geraldine Finn. Montreal: Black Rose Books, 1982. 229–250.

Delphy, Christine. *Close to Home: A Materialist Analysis of Women's Oppression.* Trans and Ed. Diana Leonard. Amherst: University of Massacheusetts Press, 1984.

Dill, Bonnie Thornton. "Race, Class and Gender: Prospects for an All-Inclusive Sisterhood." *Feminist Studies* 9.1 (1983): 130–150.

Eisenstein, Zillah. *The Radical Future of Liberal Feminism.* New York: Longmans, 1981.

Eisenstein, Zillah. *The Color of Gender: Reimagining Democracy.* USA: University of California Press, 1994.

Enloe, Cynthia. *Bananas, Beaches and Bases: Making Feminist Sense of International Politics.* Los Angeles: University of California Press, 1990.

Evans, Sara. "The Politics of Liberal Feminism." *Social Science Quarterly* 64.4 (1983): 880–897.

Firestone, Shulamith. *The Dialectic of Sex: The Case for Feminist Revolution.* New York: William Morrow, 1970.

Frankenberg, Ruth. *White Women, Race Matters: The Social Construction of Whiteness.* Minneapolis: Minnesota Press, 1993.

Fraser, Nancy. "Talking About Needs: Interpretive Contests as Political Conflicts in Welfare-State Societies." *Ethics* 99.2 (January 1989): 291–313.

French, Marilyn. *The War Against Women.* New York: Ballantine Books, 1992.

German, Lindsey. *Sex, Class and Socialism.* England: Bookmarks, 1989.

Giddings, Paula. *Where and When I Enter.* New York: William Morrow and Company Inc, 1984.

Gunew, Sneja. "Feminism and the Politics of Irreducible Differences: Multiculturalism/Ethnicity/Race." In *Feminism and the Politics.* Eds. Sneja Genew and Anna Yeatman pp. 1–23). USA: Westview Press, 1993. 1–23.

Hooks, Bell. *Ain't I a Woman?* Boston: South End Press, 1981.

Jagger, Alison. *Feminist Politics and Human Nature.* USA: Rowan & Littlefield Publishers, Inc., 1988.

Jones, Kathleen B. "Citizenship in a Woman–Friendly Polity." *Signs: Journal of Women in Culture and Society* 15.4 (1990): 781–812.

Jones, Stanlie M. "Mothering: A Possible Black Feminist Link to Social Transformation?" In *Theorizing Black Feminisms: The Visionary Pragmatism of Black Women.* Eds. Stanlie M. Jones and Abena P. A. Busia. London: Routledge, 1993. 49–63.

King, Deborah K. "Multiple Jeopardy, Multiple Consciousness: The Context of a Black Feminist Ideology." In *Feminist Theory in Practice and Process.* Ed. Micheline R. Malson. USA: University of Chicago, 1989. 75–119.

Kirby, Vicki. "Feminisms, Reading, Postmodernisms: Rethinking Complicity." In *Feminism and the Politics of Difference.* Eds. Sneja Genew and Anna Yeatman. USA: Westview Press, 1993. 24–35.

Kline, Marlee. "Women's Oppression and Racism: Critique of the Feminist Standpoint." In *Race, Class, Gender: Bonds and Barriers.* Eds. Jesse Vorst et al. Toronto: Garamond Press, 1991. 39–55.

Kreps, Bonnie. "Radical Feminism 1." In *Women Unite: An Anthology of the Canadian Women's Movement.* Toronto: Canadian Women's Educational Press, 1972. 71–75.

Laurin–Frenette, Nicole. "On the Women's Movement, Anarchism and the State." *Our Generation* 15.2 (1982): 27–39.

Miles, Angela. "Ideological Hegemony in Political Discourse: Women's Specificity and Equality." In *Feminism in Canada: From Pressure to Politics.* Eds. Angela Miles and Geraldine Finn. Montreal: Black Rose Books, 1982. 213–227.

Millet, Kate. *Sexual Politics.* New York: Avon Books, 1970.

Mohanty, Chandra Talpade. "Under Western Eyes: Feminist Scholarship and Colonial Discourses." In *Third World Women and the Politics of Feminism*. Eds. Chandra Talpade, Ann Russo and Lourdes Torres. USA: Indiana University Press, 1991. 51–80.

Molyneux, Maxine. "Women in Socialist Societies: Problems of Theory and Practice." In *Of Marriage and the Market: Women's Subordination in International Perspective*. Eds. Kate Young, Carol Wolkowitz and Rosyln McCullagh. London: CSE Books, 1981. 167–202.

Murphy, Lindsay and Jonathan Livingstone. "Racism and the Limits of Radical Feminism." *Race and Class* 36 (1985): 61–70.

Nain, Gemma Tang. "Black Women, Sexism and Racism: Black or Antiracist?" *Feminist Review* 37 (1991): 1–22.

Okin, Susan Moller. "Gender Inequalities and Cultural Differences." *Political Theory* 22.1 (1994): 5–24.

Palmer, Phyllis Marynick. "White Women/Black Women: The Dualism of Female Identity and Experience in the United States." *Feminist Studies* 9.1 (1983): 151–170.

Parmar, Pratibha. "Other Kinds of Dreams." *Feminist Review* 31 (1989): 53–65.

Pateman, Carol. *The Sexual Contract*. USA: Stanford University Press, 1988.

Pheterson, Gail. "Alliance Between Women: Overcoming Oppression and Internalized Domination." In *Bridges of Power: Women's Multicultural Alliances*. Eds. Lisa Albrecht and Rose M. Brewer. USA: New Society Publishers, 1990. 34–45.

Randall, Melanie. "Feminism and the State: Questions for Theory and Practice." *Resources for Feminist Research* 17.3 (1988): 10–16.

Russo, Ann. "We Cannot Live Without Our Lives." In *Third World Women and the Politics of Feminism*. Eds. Chandra Talpade, Ann Russo and Lourdes Torres. USA: Indiana University Press, 1991. 297–313

Sacks, Karen. *Sisters and Wives: The Past and Future of Sexual Equality*. USA: Greenwood Press, 1979.

Segal, Lynne. *Is the Future Female? Troubled Thoughts on Contemporary Feminism*. London: Virago Press, 1987.

Sen, Gita and Caren Grown. *Development, Crises, and Alternative Visions: Third World Women's Perspectives*. USA: Monthly Review Press, 1987.

Spelman, Elizabeth V. *Inessential Woman: Problems of Exclusion in Feminist Thought.* USA: Beacon Press, 1988.

Thornhill, Esmerelda. "Focus on Black Women." In *Race, Class, Gender: Bonds and Barriers.* Eds. Jesse Vorst et al. (Eds). Toronto: Garamond Press, 1991. 27–38

Tong, Rosemarie. *Feminist Thought: A Comprehensive Introduction.* USA: Westview Press, 1989.

Trimble, Linda. *Coming Soon to a Station Near You: The Process and Impact of the Canadian Radio-Telecommunication Commission's Involvement in Sex-Role Stereotyping.* Ph.D. Dissertation, Queen's University, 1990.

Wollstonecraft, Mary. *A Vindication of the Rights of Women.* USA: Penguin Books, 1992.

Yeatman, Anna. "Voice and Representation in the Politics of Difference." In *Feminism and the Politics of Difference.* Eds. Senja Genew and Anna Yeatman. USA: Westview Press, 1993. 226–241.

Young, Iris Marion. "Polity and Group Difference: A Critique of the Ideal of Universal Citizenship." *Ethics* 99.2 (January 1989): 250–274.

Young, Iris Marion. *Justice and the Politics of Difference.* New Jersey: Princeton University Press, 1990.

The First Wave of the Women's Movement

Bacchi, Carol. "Divided Allegiances: The Response of Farm and Labour Women to Suffrage." In *A Not Unreasonable Claim: Women and Reform in Canada, 1880s-1920s.* Ed. Linda Kealey. Toronto: The Women's Press, 1979. 89–107.

Bacchi, Carol. *Liberation Deferred? The Ideas of the English Canadian Suffragists, 1877-1918.* Canada: University of Toronto Press, 1983.

Bashevkin, Sylvia. "Independence Versus Partisanship: Dilemmas in the Political History of Women in English Canada". In *Rethinking Canada: The Promise of Women's History.* Eds. Veronica Strong–Boag and Anita Clair Fellman. Toronto: Copp Clark

Pitman Ltd, 1991. 415–445.

Beynon, Francis Marion. "Answers to an Anti–Suffragist". In *The Proper Sphere: Woman's Place in Canadian Society*. Eds. Ramsey Cook and Wendy Mitchinson. Toronto: Oxford University Press, 1979. 287–288.

Boutelle, Ann Edwards. "Frances Brooke's Emily Montague (1979): Canada and Women's Rights." In *Rethinking Canada: The Promise of Women's History*. Eds. Veronica Strong–Boag and Anita Clair Fellman. Toronto: Copp Clark Pitman Ltd, 1991. 51–58.

Brand, Dionne. "We Weren't Allowed to Go into Factory Work Until Hitler Started the War: The 1920s to the 1940s." In *We are Rooted Here and They Can't Pull Us Up: Essays in African Canadian Women's History*. Ed. Peggy Bristow. Toronto: University of Toronto Press, 1994. 172–193.

Bristow, Peggy. "Whatever You Raise in the Ground You Can Sell it in Chatham: Black Women in Buxton and Chatham, 1850–65." In *We Are Rooted Here and They Can't Pull Us Up: Essays in African Canadian Women's History*. Ed. Peggy Bristow. Toronto: University of Toronto Press, 1994. 68–95.

Burt, Sandra. (1994). "The Women's Movement: Working to Transform Public Life." In *The Women's Movement: Working to Transform Public Life*. Eds. James P. Bickerton and Alain G. Gagnon. Ontario: Broadview Press, 1994. 207–223.

Campbell, Gail G. "Disenfranchised but not Quiescent: Women Petitioners in New Brunswick in the Mid–Nineteenth Century." In *Rethinking Canada: The Promise of Women's History*. Eds. Veronica Strong–Boag and Anita Clair Fellman. Toronto: Copp Clark Pitman Ltd, 1991. 81–96.

Canadian Monthly and National Review. "An Argument Against Woman's Rights." In *The Proper Sphere: Woman's Place in Canadian Society*. Eds. Ramsey Cook and Wendy Mitchinson. Toronto: Oxford University Press, 1979. 34–51.

Canadian Monthly and National Review. "An Argument For Women's Rights." In *The Proper Sphere: Woman's Place in Canadian Society*. Eds. Ramsey Cook and Wendy Mitchinson. Toronto: Oxford University Press, 1979. 51–64

Carty, Linda. "African Canadian Women and the State: Labour

Only Please". In *We Are Rooted Here and They Can't Pull Us Up: Essays in African Canadian Women's History.* Ed. Peggy Bristow. Toronto: University of Toronto Press, 1994. 194–221.

Conrad, Margaret. "'Sundays Always Make Me Think of Home': Time and Place in Canadian Women's History." In *Rethinking Canada: The Promise of Women's History.* Eds. Veronica Strong–Boag and Anita Clair Fellman. Toronto: Copp Clark Pitman Ltd, 1991. 97–112.

Cook, Ramsey and Wendy Mitchinson, Eds. *The Proper Sphere: Woman's Place in Canadian Society.* Toronto: Oxford University Press, 1979.

Errington, Jane. "Pioneers and Suffragists." In *Changing Patterns: Women in Canada.* Eds. Sandra Burt, Lorraine Code and Lindsay Dorney. Toronto: McClelland & Stewart, 1990. 51–79.

Gorham, Deborah. "The Canadian Suffragists." In *Women in the Canadian Mosaic.* Ed. Gwen Matheson. Toronto: Peter Martin Associates Limited, 1976. 23–55.

Gorham, Deborah. "Flora MacDonald Denison: Canadian Feminist." In *A Not Unreasonable Claim: Women and Reform in Canada, 1880s-1920s.* Ed. Linda Kealey. Toronto: The Women's Press, 1979. 47–70.

Grant, Gordon Mrs. "The Vote to do Away with Drink." In *The Proper Sphere: Woman's Place in Canadian Society.* Eds. Ramsey Cook and Wendy Mitchinson. Toronto: Oxford University Press, 1979. 256–258

Hamilton, Sylvia. "Naming Names, Naming Ourselves: A Survey of Early Black Women in Nova Scotia." In *We Are Rooted Here and They Can't Pull Us Up: Essays in African Canadian Women's History.* Ed. Peggy Bristow. Toronto: University of Toronto Press, 1994. 13–38.

Hughes, James L. "Equal Suffrage." In *The Proper Sphere: Woman's Place in Canadian Society.* Eds. Ramsey Cook and Wendy Mitchinson. Toronto: Oxford University Press, 1979. 266–287.

Kealey, Linda. "Introduction." In *A Not Unreasonable Claim: Women and Reform in Canada, 1880s-1920s.* Ed. Linda Kealey. Toronto: The Women's Press, 1979. 1–14.

Leathes, Sonia. "Votes for Women–An Argument in Favor." In *The*

Proper Sphere: Woman's Place in Canadian Society. Eds. Ramsey Cook and Wendy Mitchinson. Toronto: Oxford University Press, 1979. 293–300.

Macphail, Andrew. "Votes for Women–An Argument Against." In *The Proper Sphere: Woman's Place in Canadian Society*. Eds. Ramsey Cook and Wendy Mitchinson. Toronto: Oxford University Press, 1979. 300–309.

Mahood, Sally. "The Women's Suffrage Movement in Canada and Saskatchewan". In *Women Unite: An Anthology of the Canadian Women's Movement*. Toronto: Canadian Women's Educational Press, 1972. 21–30.

Matheson, Gwen and V. E. Lang. "Nellie McClung: Not a Nice Woman." In *Women in the Canadian Mosaic*. Ed. Gwen Matheson. Toronto: Peter Martin Associates Limited, 1976. 1–20.

McClung, Nellie. "What Women Will Do with the Vote." In *The Proper Sphere: Woman's Place in Canadian Society*. Eds. Ramsey Cook and Wendy Mitchinson. Toronto: Oxford University Press, 1979. 319–324.

McClung, Nellie. "Women are Discontented." In *The Proper Sphere: Woman's Place in Canadian Society*. Eds. Ramsey Cook and Wendy Mitchinson. Toronto: Oxford University Press, 1979. 288–293.

McClung, Nellie. "Votes for Women–A Suffragist Speaks." In *The Proper Sphere: Woman's Place in Canadian Society*. Eds. Ramsey Cook and Wendy Mitchinson. Toronto: Oxford University Press, 1979. 313–319.

Mitchinson, Wendy. "The WCTU: 'For God Home and Native Land': A Study in Nineteenth–Century Feminism." In *A Not Unreasonable Claim: Women and Reform in Canada, 1880s-1920s*. Ed. Linda Kealey. Toronto: The Women's Press, 1979. 151–167.

National Council of Women of Canada. "Education for Domesticity." In *The Proper Sphere: Woman's Place in Canadian Society*. Eds. Ramsey Cook and Wendy Mitchinson. Toronto: Oxford University Press, 1979. 149–155.

Newton, Janice. *The Feminist Challenge to the Canadian Left, 1900-1918*. Canada: McGill–Queen's University Press, 1995.

Noel, Jan. "New France: Les Femmes Favoritisées." In *Rethinking Canada: The Promise of Women's History*. Eds. Veronica Strong–

Boag and Anita Clair. Toronto: Copp Clark Pitman Ltd, 1991. 28–50

Parker, Helen Cameron. "Training for Housework." In *The Proper Sphere: Woman's Place in Canadian Society*. Eds. Ramsey Cook and Wendy Mitchinson. Toronto: Oxford University Press, 1979. 145–149.

Parker, Mrs. Dr. "Woman in Nation-Building." In *The Proper Sphere: Woman's Place in Canadian Society*. Eds. Ramsey Cook and Wendy Mitchinson. Toronto: Oxford University Press, 1979. 226–230.

Potter, Janice. "Patriarchy and Paternalism: The Case of Eastern European Ontario Loyalist Women." In *Rethinking Canada: The Promise of Women's History*. Eds. Veronica Strong–Boag and Anita Clair Fellman. Toronto: Copp Clark Pitman Ltd, 1991. 59–72.

Roberts, Barbara. "'A Work of Empire': Canadian Reformers and British Female Immigration." In *A Not Unreasonable Claim: Women and Reform in Canada, 1880s-1920s*. Ed. Linda Kealey. Toronto: The Women's Press, 1979. 185–201.

Roberts, Wayne. "Rocking the Cradle for the World: The New Woman and Maternal Feminism." In *A Not Unreasonable Claim: Women and Reform in Canada, 1880s-1920s*. Ed. Linda Kealey. Toronto: The Women's Press, 1979. 15–45.

Sedgewick, Robert. "Woman's Sphere." In *The Proper Sphere: Woman's Place in Canadian Society*. Ed. Ramsey Cook and Wendy Mitchinson. Toronto: Oxford University Press, 1979. 8–34.

Shadd, Adrienne. "The Lord Seemed to Say Go: Women and the Underground Railroad Movement." In *We Are Rooted Here and They Can't Pull Us Up: Essays in African Canadian Women's History*. Ed. Peggy Bristow. Toronto: University of Toronto Press, 1994. 39–67.

Stowe-Gullen, Dr. "A Woman is a Citizen." In *The Proper Sphere: Woman's Place in Canadian Society*. Eds. Ramsey Cook and Wendy Mitchinson. Toronto: Oxford University Press, 1979. 258–264.

Strong–Boag, Veronica. "'Ever a Crusader': Nellie McClung, First-Wave Feminist." In *Rethinking Canada: The Promise of Women's History*. Eds. Veronica Strong–Boag and Anita Clair Fellman. Toronto: Copp Clark Pitman Ltd, 1991. 308–321.

Women's Christian Temperance Union. "Demands for Municipal

Franchise." In *The Proper Sphere: Woman's Place in Canadian Society*. Eds. Ramsey Cook and Wendy Mitchinson. Toronto: Oxford University Press, 1979. 265–266.

The Second Wave of the Women's Movement

Adamson, Nancy, Linda Briskin and Margaret McPhail. *Feminists Organizing for Change: The Contemporary Women's Movement in Canada*. Toronto: Oxford University Press, 1988.

Armstrong, Pat and Hugh. *The Double Ghetto: Canadian Women and Their Segregated Work*. Toronto: McClelland & Stewart, 1984.

Bashevkin, Sylvia. "Confronting Neo-Conservatism: Anglo-American Women's Movements under Thatcher, Reagan and Mulroney." *International Political Science Review* 15.3 (1994): 275–296.

Bashevkin, Sylvia. "Building a Political Voice: Women's Participation and Policy Influence in Canada." In *Woman and Politics Worldwide*. Eds. Barbara J. Nelson and Najma Chowdhury. USA: Yale University Press, 1994. 143–160.

Bégin, Monique. "The Royal Commission on the Status of Women in Canada: Twenty Years Later." In *Challenging Times: The Women's Movement in Canada and the United States*. Eds. Constance Backhouse and David Flaherty. Canada: McGill-Queen's University Press, 1992. 21–38.

Berstein, Judy, Peggy Morton, Linda Seese and Myrna Wood. "Sisters, Brothers, Lovers...Listen..." In *Women Unite: An Anthology of the Canadian Women's Movement*. Toronto: Canadian Women's Educational Press, 1972. 31–39.

Brodie, Janine. *Politics on the Boundaries: Restructuring and the Canadian Women's Movement*. Toronto: Robarts Center for Canadian Studies, 1994.

Brodie, Janine. *Politics on the Margins: Restructuring and the Canadian Women's Movement*. Nova Scotia: Fernwood Publishing Company, 1995.

Brown, Rosemary. "A New Kind of Power." In *Women in the Canadian Mosaic*. Ed. Gwen Matheson. Toronto: Peter Martin Associates Limited, 1976. 289–298.

Cameron, Barb and Cathy Pike. "Collective Child Care in a Class Society." In *Women Unite: An Anthology of the Canadian Women's Movement*. Toronto: Canadian Women's Educational Press, 1972. 87–89.

Carty, Linda and Dionne Brand. "'Visible Minority' Women – A Creation of the Canadian State." *Resources for Feminist Research* 17.3 (1988): 39–42.

Carty, Linda. "Combining Our Efforts: Making Feminism Relevant to the Changing Sociality." In *And Still We Rise: Feminist Political Mobilizing in Contemporary Canada*. Ed. Linda Carty. Toronto: The Women's Press, 1993. 7–21.

Findlay, Sue. "Problematizing Privilege: Another Look at Representation of 'Women'." In *And Still We Rise: Feminist Political Mobilizing in Contemporary Canada*. Ed. Linda Carty. Toronto: The Women's Press, 1993. 207–223.

Gottlieb, Amy (Ed.). "What About Us? Organizing Inclusively in the National Action Committee on the Status of Women – A Roundtable Discussion Facilitated by Maureen FitzGerald and Amy de Wolff." In *And Still We Rise: Feminist Political Mobilizing in Contemporary Canada*. Ed. Linda Carty. Toronto: The Women's Press, 1993. 371–385.

James, Alice. "Poverty: Canada's Legacy to Women." In *Women Unite: An Anthology of the Canadian Women's Movement*. Toronto: Canadian Women's Educational Press, 1972. 121–140.

Kantaroff, Maryon. "Breaking Out of the Female Mould." In *Women in the Canadian Mosaic*. Ed. Gwen Matheson. Toronto: Peter Martin Associates Limited, 1976. 275–287.

Lillian, Melody. "Children are Only Littler People...Or the Louis Riel University Family Co-op." In *Women Unite: An Anthology of the Canadian Women's Movement*. Toronto: Canadian Women's Educational Press, 1972. 90–99.

Macpherson, Kay and Meg Sears. "The Voice of Women: A History." In *Women in the Canadian Mosaic*. Ed. Gwen Matheson. Toronto: Peter Martin Associates Limited, 1976. 71–89.

Macpherson, Kay. "Politics Within the Women's Movement." *Status of Women News* 5.4 (Summer 1979): 6–7.

McBride, Stephen. "Hard Times and the 'Rules of the Game': A Study of the Legislative Environment of Labour–Capital Conflict." In *Working People and Hard Times*. Eds. Robert Argue, Charlene Gannagé and D. W. Livingstone. Toronto: Garamond Press, 1987. 98–111.

McDowell, Linda and Rosemary Pringle, Eds. *Defining Women: Social Institutions and Gender_Divisions*. United Kingdom: Polity Press, 1992.

McKensie, Maxine. "You Mean I Still Ain't?" *Breaking the Silence* 5.3 (Spring 1987): 8–9.

Morris, Cerise. "'Determination and Thoroughness': The Movement for a Royal Commission on the Status of Women in Canada." *Atlantis* 5.2 (1980): 1–21.

Morris, Cerise. "Pressuring the Canadian State for Women's Rights: The Role of the National Action Committee on the Status of Women." *Alternate Routes* 6 (1983): 87–108.

Morton, Peggy. "Women's Work is Never Done...Or the Production, Maintenance and Reproduction of Labour Power." In *Women Unite: An Anthology of the Canadian Women's Movement*. Toronto: Canadian Women's Educational Press, 1972.

Nemiroff, Greta Hofmann and Susan McCrae van der Voet. "Feminist Research: Does it Affect Government Policy?" *Communiqu'elles* 11.1 (January 1985): 13–22.

Ng, Roxana. "Immigrant Women and Institutionalized Racism." In *Changing Patterns: Women in Canada*. Eds. Sandra Burt, Lorraine Code and Lindsay Dorney. Canada: McClelland & Stewart Inc, 1990. 184–203.

Ng, Roxana. "Sexism, Racism and Canadian Nationalism." In *Feminism and the Politics of Difference*. Eds. Sneja Genew and Anna Yeatman. USA: Westview Press, 1993. 197–207.

Pierson, Ruth Roach. "The Politics of the Domestic Sphere." In *Canadian Women's Issues: Volume II*. Eds. Ruth Roach Pierson and Marjorie Griffin Cohen. Toronto: James Lorimer & Company, 1995. 1–33.

Rands, Jean. "Towards an Organization of Working Women." In

Women Unite: An Anthology of the Canadian Women's Movement. Toronto: Canadian Women's Educational Press, 1972.

Rebick, Judy. "Unity in Diversity: The Women's Movement in Canada." *Social Policy* (Summer 1992): 47–55.

Simms, Glenda. "Beyond the White Veil." In *Challenging Times: The Women's Movement in Canada and the United States.* Eds. Constance Backhouse and David Flaherty. Montreal: McGill–Queen's University Press, 1992. 175–181.

Status of Women Canada. *Setting the Stage for the Next Century: The Federal Plan for Gender Equity.* Canada: Status of Women Canada, 1995.

Status of Women Canada. *Women's Equality in Canada: Progress in Implementing the Nairobi Forward-Looking Strategies for the Advancement of Women.* Canada: Status of Women Canada, 1995.

Teather, Lynne. "The Feminist Mosaic." In *Women in the Canadian Mosaic.* Ed. Gwen Matheson. Toronto: Peter Martin Associates Limited, 1976. 301–346.

Vickers, Jill. "The Intellectual Origins of the Women's Movements in Canada." In *Challenging Times: The Women's Movement in Canada and the United States.* Eds. Constance Backhouse and David Flaherty. Canada: McGill–Queen's University Press, 1992. 39–60.

Vickers, Jill, Pauline Rankin and Christine Appelle. *Politics as if Women Mattered: A Political Analysis of the National Action Committee on the Status of Women.* Toronto: University of Toronto Press, 1993.

Immigration Policy Concerning Foreign Domestic Workers

Anderson, Grace M. and William Marr. "Immigration and Social Policy." In *Canadian Social Policy.* Ed. Shankar A. Yelaja. Canada: Wilfred Laurier Press, 1987. 88–113.

Arat-Koc, Sedef. "In the Privacy of Our Own Home: Foreign Domestic Workers as the Solution to the Crisis in the

Domestic Sphere in Canada." *Studies in Political Economy* 28 (Spring 1989): 22–58.

l'Association pour la défense des droits du personnel domestique de Montréal. *Mémoire présenté à Madame Louise Harel, Ministre de l'Emploi.* Québec: January 1995.

AWARE. *Newsletter.* Canada: April–June, 1993.

AWARE. *Newsletter.* Canada: Summer, 1993.

AWARE. *Newsletter.* Canada: Winter, 1994.

Bakan, Abigail and Daiva K. Stasiulis. "Foreign Domestic Worker Policy in Canada and the Social Boundaries of Modern Citizenship." *Science and Society* 58.1 (Spring 1994): 7–33.

Bakan, Abigail and Daiva K. Stasiulis. "Making the Match: Domestic Placement Agencies and the Racialization of Women's Household Work." *Signs: Journal of Women in Culture and Society* 20.21 (Winter 1995): 303–335.

Breti, Diana and Christina Davidson. *Foreign Domestic Workers in British Columbia.* Background Paper: West Coast Domestic Workers' Association, July 1989.

Calliste, Agnes. "Canada's Immigration Policy and Domestics from the Caribbean: The Second Domestic Scheme." In *Race, Class and Gender: Bonds and Barriers.* Ed. Jesse Vorste. Toronto: Garamond Press, 1991. 136–169.

Calliste, Agnes. "Race, Gender and Canadian Immigration Policy: Blacks from the Caribbean, 1900–1932." *Journal of Canadian Studies* 28.4 (Winter 1993–1994): 131–148.

Center for Women's Resources. *PIGLAS-DIWA: Issues and Trends about Women of the Philippines — Migrant Women.* Philippines: July–September, 1989.

Center for Women's Resources. *Usaping Lila.* Philippines: July 1993.

Cohen, Rina. "A Brief History of Racism in Immigration Policies for Recruiting Domestics." *Canadian Women Studies* 14. 2 (1994): 83–86.

Daenzer, Patricia. *Regulating Class Privilege: Immigrant Servants in Canada, 1940s-1990s.* Toronto: Canadian Scholars Press, 1993.

Estable, Alma. "Immigrant Women: From the Outside Looking In." *Breaking the Silence* 4. 3/4 (Spring/Summer 1986): 10–11.

Foster, John. "Sussex Day Care." In *Women Unite: An Anthology of the*

Canadian Women's Movement. Toronto: Canadian Women's Educational Press, 1972. 99–108.

Gardiner, Susan. "Women's Domestic Labour." *New Left Review* 89 (1975): 47–58.

Harder, Lois. "The Trouble with Democracy: Child Care in Ontario and the Politics of Representation." In *And Still We Rise: Feminist Political Mobilizing in Contemporary Canada*. Ed. Linda Carty. Toronto: The Women's Press, 1993. 243–257.

Harris, Ruth Lynette. *The Transformation of Canadian Policies and Programs to Recruit Foreign Labour: The Case of Caribbean Female Domestic Workers, 1950s-1990s*. Ph.D. Dissertation: Michigan State University, 1988.

IBON. *The Crisis of Philippine Labour Migration*. Manila: May, 1995.

INTERCEDE. *Domestics' Cross-Cultural News*. Toronto: February 1990.

INTERCEDE. *Domestics' Cross-Cultural News*. Toronto: December 1990.

MATCH International Center. *Match News*. Ottawa: Fall 1992.

MATCH International Center. *Match News*. Ottawa: Spring 1993.

Migrant Forum in Asia. *Protecting Migrant Workers*. Hong Kong: 1994.

Ottawa Multicultural Homemakers Association. *Letter of Appeal to Minister Barbara McDougall RE: Federal Review of the Foreign Domestic Workers Program*. Ottawa: January 19, 1990.

Rojas, Henry S. "Filipino Labour Export: An Initial Critique." Draft by the Executive Director of KAIBIGAN, 1994.

Satzewich, Vic. "Racism and Canadian Immigration Policy: The Government's View of Caribbean Migration, 1962–1966." *Canadian Ethnic Studies* 21.1 (1989): 77–97.

Ship, Susan Judith. "Au–délà de la solidarité feminine." *Politique* 19 (1991): 5–36.

Silvera, Makeda. *Silenced*. Toronto: Sister Vision, 1989.

Smith, Michelle and Marie Boti. *Exporting Lives: Stories of Filipina Migrant Workers in Canada and the Philippines*. Montreal: Center for Philippine Concerns' Women's Committee, 1995.

Villasin, Felicita O. and M. Ann Phillips. "Falling Through the Cracks: Domestic Workers and Progressive Movements." *Canadian Woman Studies* 14.2 (1994): 87–90.

West Coast Domestic Workers' Association. *Brief to the Review Committee on the Foreign Domestic Worker Program.* Vancouver: November 1989.

West Coast Domestic Workers' Association. *Newsletter* 3.1. Vancouver: January 1990.

West Coast Domestic Workers' Association. *Newsletter* 3.4. Vancouver: April 1990.

West Coast Domestic Workers' Association. *Newsletter* 4.2. Vancouver: February 1991.

Index

BLACK ROSE BOOKS

has also published the following books of related interest

Aphra Behn: The English Sappho, *by George Woodcock*
Balance: Art and Nature, *by John Grande*
Beyond Boundaries, *by Barbara Noske*
Female Parts: The Art and Politics of Women Playrights, *by Yvonne Hodkinson*
Finding Our Way: Rethinking Eco-Feminist Politics, *by Janet Biehl*
History of Canadian Business 1867-1914, *by R. T. Naylor*
Killing Hope: US Military and CIA Interventions Since World War II, *by William Blum*
Military in Greek Politics, *by Thanos Veremis*
Nationalism and Culture, *by Rudolf Rocker*
Philosophy of Social Ecology, *by Murray Bookchin*
Politics of Social Ecology, *by Janet Biehl and Murray Bookchin*
Politics of Individualism: Liberalism, Liberal Feminism and Anarchism, *by L. Susan Brown*
Politics of Obedience, *by Etienne de la Boétie*
Politics of Sustainable Development, *by Laurie E. Adkin*
Regulation of Desire: Homo and Hetero Sexualities, *by Gary Kinsman*
Triumph of the Market, *by Edward S. Herman*
Women Pirates and the Politics of the Jolly Roger, *by Ulrike Klausmann, Marion Meinzerin,*
    Gabriel Kuhn
Women and Religion, *by Fatmagül Berktay*
Zapata of Mexico, *by Peter Newell*

send for a free catalogue of all our titles
BLACK ROSE BOOKS
C.P. 1258
Succ. Place du Parc
Montréal, Québec
H3W 2R3 Canada

To order books in North America: (phone) 1-800-565-9523
(fax) 1-800-221-9985
In Europe: (phone) 44-081-986-4854 (fax) 44-081-533-5821

Web site address: http://www.web.net/blackrosebooks

Printed by the workers of
VEILLEUX IMPRESSION À DEMANDE INC.
Boucherville, Quebec
for Black Rose Books Ltd.